THE POWER OF THE OTHER

ALSO BY HENRY CLOUD

Necessary Endings

Integrity

Boundaries for Leaders

Boundaries

The One-Life Solution

9 Things You Simply Must Do to Succeed in Love and Life

9 Things a Leader Must Do

THE POWER OF THE OTHER

THE STARTLING EFFECT OTHER PEOPLE HAVE ON YOU, FROM THE BOARDROOM TO THE BEDROOM AND BEYOND—AND WHAT TO DO ABOUT IT

DR. HENRY CLOUD

HARPER
BUSINESS

An Imprint of HarperCollinsPublishers

HarperCollins books may be purchased for educational, business, or sales promotional use. For information, please e-mail the Special Markets Department at SPsales@harpercollins.com.

FIRST EDITION

Library of Congress Cataloging-in-Publication Data has been applied for.

ISBN: 978-0-06-177714-1 (Hardcover)
ISBN: 978-0-06-249958-5 (International Edition)

16 17 18 19 20   ov/rrd   10 9 8 7 6 5 4 3 2

This book is dedicated to all of the "others" whose power has saved and enriched my life. I will be forever grateful.

CONTENTS

THE POWER OF THE OTHER

THE NEGLECTED TRUTH

Human performance, *your* performance, has its limits. Or does it?

In large measure, that question is the focus of this book—not so much whether there *are* limits, as that is almost an unknowable question. After all, who knows what the real human limits are? Every time we think someone reaches one, someone else surpasses what we thought was the apex. What we think is the known limit is always being redefined, even for ourselves.

Our focus here will be on how and why some people are able to surpass limits. In my work with executives and high-performance organizations, this is the issue we address, in one of two forms.

The first form involves some *known* limit my clients are experiencing: a pattern, an obstacle, a leadership dilemma or challenge, a conflict with a person, a weakness, or problem—something that they know is getting in the way, blocking their desired future, their business, or even threatening their lives. *Something* is limiting them . . . even if they don't know exactly what it is.

The second form doesn't involve a known problem or issue at all. There is just the desire to get better, to grow past a current level, to have or do *more*: more potential, more profits, more horsepower, more fun, more meaning, more love, . . . more joy. These clients know there is more to be had within themselves, their business, or their lives. And they want it.

You may have already identified the issue keeping you from the next level of performance, or you just want to make sure you get as far as you can go. In either case, you want to surpass your current limit, your current reality. How that is actually done is the subject of this book: **how we become *better*, how we become *more*.**

And here's the good news: it's not a mystery. We know how it happens. Better yet, you can learn how.

MORE WHEN THERE IS NO MORE

When members of the U.S. Navy become Navy SEALs, they don't win a lottery. In one of most performance-driven selection processes in the world, they earn it. Selected from the top of the top of the top, applicants must be the best of the best at every step along the way. There are no favors. They must perform in a true meritocracy.

There are many steps, many qualifications, and many gates that must be passed through to get to the final stages of the selection process. Toward the end of the training program, called

BUDS (Basic Underwater Demolition SEAL) training, the aspiring SEALs must pass the test of all tests—"Hell Week," a grueling exercise requiring the utmost physical and mental endurance, pushing these already-at-the-top specimens to their absolute limits.

Enduring near-hypothermia in cold water, long-distance swims during sleep deprivation, and intense physical strain, more than two thirds of the candidates don't make it through the training. And remember, they are all the best of the best. Most ultimately "ring the bell," signaling that they have given up. But actually they have rarely given up, for they still *want* it desperately. It is more that their bodies and their minds have hit the limit of their capabilities. There is no more to give, no way to do better. Whether it is physical pain, mental exhaustion, or both, most candidates lack the resources that will allow them to surpass their own limits and reach the next step, the toughest one required to become a SEAL. The entire selection process is set up to find out exactly where those limits are, who has them, and who can surpass them. The ones who make it through the process of pushing these limits are the ones who are sent out into battles that require humans to perform past normal limits on a regular basis. Life or death and victory or defeat depend on that very ability.

My brother-in-law Mark was a Navy SEAL. He made it through BUDS successfully. Mark was the brother I never had (I had two sisters), the kind of brother every kid wants. I used to love to hear his stories (the ones he could tell me without having to kill me) about the extraordinary feats he and his fellow SEALs would routinely pull off: jumping out of an airplane at crazy altitudes, hitting the surface of a cold ocean in some faraway land, changing into battle gear, taking a power nap on the ocean floor, and then boarding an enemy ship in the darkness and taking it down. And then asking, after all that, "So what's for lunch?" as if it were just another day at work. Routines that none of the rest of us could think of enduring, much less succeeding at. Incredible.

We lost Mark in the Iraq war. He died a hero's death, doing exactly what he loved: using his skills, with his team of comrades, to fight for our country and deliver people to safety who had been captured by terrorists. It was a beyond-devastating blow for all of us who loved and admired him, and we felt deep appreciation for the sacrificial person that he was. He left his wife and infant daughter behind, a large extended family, and many friends whose lives he had touched.

In the aftermath of his death, I got to meet many of his SEAL team members, colleagues and comrades, most of whom had fought side by side with him in Afghanistan and Iraq. They shared stories of Mark's courage, skills, personality, spirit, and love of life. He had left a mark on many, many lives. We were one big community of those who were touched by him, grieving, remembering, and celebrating together, sharing memories and stories.

The story that relates to our topic here is one of the clearest examples I know of how human limits, when encountered, are surpassed. It was relayed by one of Mark's SEAL team members in the days after his death.

His teammate, whom I'll call Bryce, was in the ocean during Hell Week, swimming the last long leg to the finish line. Mark had already made it; he had passed the final test and knew that he would become a SEAL. For him, it was done, and he was standing on the rocks above the water, eagerly watching his buddies strive toward the goal.

That was when Bryce "hit the wall."

As he described it, it was that moment when his body would just go no more. It was done. Nothing left. He tried to will himself to keep going, but his body would not obey.

Maybe you can relate to this in some way. If you have ever been to the gym and lifted a weight for enough repetitions over and over, you got to that same point: your arms were done. No more. There was nothing left to give, no surge of will that would make them do one more rep.

That was where Bryce found himself at that moment, beginning to sink in the cold water, totally out of fuel, strength, or the ability to go another yard. Push as he would, strain as he would, his body and his skills were failing him.

Imagine that moment: all of those years, all of that training, all of that sacrifice . . . about to be gone. He could see his dreams sinking with him, about to be over. What must it have felt like, to have gone through everything he had gone through to make it up to the very end? I am sure that the lights were going out in his heart, as his body would go no further. Until . . .

As he told the story of going down, about to call for help and signal that it was over for him, his eyes fell upon the land ahead. There was Mark, standing on the shore. Mark saw him, and Bryce said that Mark gave him a huge fist pump and a yell, signaling to Bryce that "he could do it." Their eyes locked for a few seconds, and as Bryce described it, *something* happened. *Something beyond him.* His body jumped into another gear, into another dimension of performance that he had not had access to before; he was able to get back on top of the cold water again and swim toward the finish line. He made it. He finished. He would be a SEAL.

That is the "power of the other."

THE MYSTERY AND THE CERTAINTY

What happened? Why was a look and a fist pump from a friend able to lift Bryce past his physical and mental limits? Why did his body get on top of the water again, almost on autopilot? Why did his arms and legs find *more* than they had before?

In some ways, we don't know. How can something as immaterial, invisible, and mystical as an emotional connection with a buddy have what amounts to a material, measureable, and physical effect like fueling a body across space and physical boundaries? It's very elusive.

For centuries, philosophers, psychologists, theologians, and spiritual thinkers have struggled with something called the mind-body problem, the fact that the *invisible* has a real effect on the *visible*, and vice versa. But however we explain these mechanisms, the neglected truth is that the invisible attributes of relationship, the **connection** between people, have real, tangible, and measurable power.

It begins at birth. Did you know that even if you feed babies but deprive them of meaningful relational connections, an attachment or bond, they will not grow as they should? Just from missing a relational connection? They will have lower body weights, experience more illness, and in extreme situations, they can develop a syndrome called failure to thrive. It is a term that means exactly that; they are hitting a *false* limit. They are not thriving to their full physical potential.

The damage from a lack of connection goes even deeper. It is not just what we can see on the outside. If you were to look at their brains on brain scans, as many researchers have done, you'll see literal black holes, spaces where the neurons did not form, where neurological systems did not grow; the physical hard-wiring of their brains is incomplete. Indeed, children who've experienced these deprivations often have smaller brains, too. That's why we see behavior deficits and performance problems later. These kids are trying to meet the demands of reality without the circuitry needed to do so. *And the reason they have those limits is the lack of relationship, of human connection.*

But the need for connection begins even before birth. It goes literally from the womb to the tomb. Relationship affects our physical and mental functioning throughout life. This invisible power, the power of the other, builds both the hardware and the software that leads to healthy functioning and better performance. For example, research shows over and over again that people trying to reach goals succeed at a much greater rate if they are connected to a strong human support system. Similarly, research shows that elderly who have suffered heart attacks or strokes fare much better, with lower incidence of recurrence, when they join a support group. Other research has shown that people who tap into the power of the other have stronger immune systems, tend to get sick less frequently, and recover faster when they do. Even if you eat an unhealthy diet but are part of a close-knit community, you will live longer than if you are emotionally isolated and eat only healthy foods. (I say amen to that!)

We can wonder how it happens and why, and strive to figure it out. But we can no longer dispute that it does happen. Relationship affects life and performance, period. So in this book, let's talk about that, and how it really works.

A DIFFERENT CONVERSATION

I am a psychologist, leadership consultant, and coach. By definition, my work focuses on human performance, how people—individuals, teams, and organizations—can do better. If you are a student of performance growth, whether in business or personal life, you might have noticed that the conversation about how *we* do better is all about *you*.

Improve *your* techniques, *your* thinking, *your* strategies and skills. Intensify *your* discipline. Clarify *your* goals, *your* commitment, *your* communication. There are many other skills, tactics, strategies, competencies, and abilities that you must increase and improve in order to get there. In short, the message is "You can do it! You can get more by getting better." Learn more, do this, think differently, lead in a different way. You can succeed by being a better you.

Guess what. All of that is true. Wisdom and competency do matter. We do need new skills, knowledge, and ability. We must strive to become better versions of ourselves in order to do better and be more than we are.

But there is something missing from that menu: *reality*.

Ask many people about their greatest accomplishments and challenges overcome, and you will find one thing in common: **there was someone on the other end who made it possible.**

Both your best and worst seasons were not just about the market or the business cycle, or even your own skills. Your best and worst seasons were also about *who* was in that season with you. Either for good or bad. It was not just about you. It was about the others who were playing a big part in whom you were becoming and how you were doing.

This book represents a major shift in the conversation on leadership, growth, and high performance. I want to shift the conversation from a focus only on *you* (i.e., here is how *you* can develop yourself) to a recognition that *your own performance is either improved or diminished by the other people in your scenario.* They hold power. Whereas most leadership advice and most business books focus on how you lead others, how you perform, and how you build your skills and competencies, this book will focus on the people—those others—who affect you and on the power you have as an other for them.

The undeniable reality is that how well you do in life and in business depends not only on what you do and how you do it, your skills and competencies, but also on who is doing it *with* you or *to* you. Who is helping you? Who is fighting you? Who is strengthening you or resisting and diminishing you? These people are literally making you who you are. Who is helping you build those skills and competencies? Who is tearing them down? Other people *do* have power in your life, for good or bad. But what *kind* of power are others going to have over your life and performance? Are they going to enhance or diminish? These are the questions we will examine.

You don't have a choice about whether or not others have power in your life. They do. But you do have a choice as to what kind of power others are going to have.

How many times have you seen or experienced the power that a boss has—either to help you or to stifle or wreck your vision? A direct report, a coworker, a partner, a fellow board member can help you or hinder you. How many times have you seen the power of others get in the way? How many times have you seen one person ruin the atmosphere or culture of a team, a circle of friends, or a family? And how many times have you seen a situation, or your life, get turned around because the right person showed up? Other people play a role at every step. They influence you as much as you influence them.

How you manage this power is the difference between winning and losing, between succeeding and failing to thrive. Whom you trust, whom you don't, what you get from others, and how you deal with them will determine everything. You can't master people, but you can become a master at choosing and dealing with people.

When you get the power of the other on your side, you can surpass whatever limit you are currently experiencing or will ever experience in the future.

CHAPTER TWO

THE SCIENCE OF CONNECTION

The emotional impact on me was so powerfully negative that I will never forget that moment, that day in class.

When I was in college, I had been totally into accounting and finance, but after going through some big life changes, in my third year, I began a race to prepare for a career in psychology. It was to be my life mission. I took every course I could, speeding to try to learn it all, even before entering graduate school. I was really excited about studying the science behind how we thrive, function, perform, and are healed. There would be so much to learn. I looked forward to becoming an expert and having a life purpose and mission of helping others. I wanted to become the best "doc" that I could become and learn all of the best treatment protocols, coaching and consulting methodologies, and anything

else that would add to my toolbox. By the time I left for graduate school three years later, even apart from my college psychology
classes, I had gone for training in cognitive therapy, Gestalt psychology, transactional analysis, organizational behavior, behavioral
interventions, group therapy, primal therapy, psychodynamic treatment, inpatient treatment, and several aspects of spiritual development. Being a bit obsessive, as you can gather, I was on a mission to
learn everything I could.

Then, in the midst of all that excitement, one day I got so discouraged, I almost wanted to go back to studying finance. It was in
a class where the professor was reviewing a meta-analysis of clinical
psychology's treatments—a summation of what methods of treatment worked the best. A team of researchers had "factor analyzed"
all of the different treatment outcomes in order to understand
what it was that really produced change, growth, and healing in a
person. The researchers looked at each technique's style, interventions on thinking and feelings, dynamics, and the like. While all of
that was important, my professor explained, there was something
else, some other factor that had really produced *the* curative force
across each of these modalities. There was *one* thing that actually
brought about the change.

I sat eagerly, waiting to find out the secret of helping people.
Here, at last, I would learn that esoteric kernel of wisdom that I
had been seeking all of this time. The professor looked at us and
said, "It's the relationship. What actually brings about change in
people, and the cure, is the relationship between the psychologist
and the client," he explained.

"*What?*" I thought to myself. "That's *it*? That's all there is? *That's*
what I gave up finance and law school for? To be a "rent-a-friend?"

The wind had been knocked out of me. I could go through all of this training, graduate school, internships, and the rest, learn all of this stuff, and really all that would matter is the *relationship?* Then why the hell am I doing this? What this guy is saying is that my fraternity is basically a treatment center. We have relationships there, but doesn't he know we have a lot of crazy behavior, too? Is he suggesting that all you need is a friend?

There has to be something wrong with this, I remember thinking. But there it was: the science had shown that it was the *relationship* that was the curative factor.

I don't recall the rest of the lecture, but I continued past that fateful, demoralizing day even though I had just been told that everything I would learn over the next seven years of training would not be worth much more than what my pals had already given me. It couldn't be true.

But I ended up learning that the research results were actually 100 percent true. And 100 percent *not.*

How can that be?

Science confirms that getting to the next level *is* 100 percent dependent on relationship. But . . . the relationship must be the right *kind* of relationship, more than just hanging out with pals. The relationship must provide very specific functions and very specific energy; it must deliver very specific constructive experiences and encode very specific information within the brains of those in the relationship. The right kinds of relationships wire us for resilience and success. In this book, we will look at what relationships that help us get to the next level must provide.

THE GEOMETRY OF RELATIONSHIPS

Daniel Siegel is a professor at UCLA and a leading neurobiologist. He is one of the scientists whose studies of the brain help elucidate how it interfaces with the aspects of life that determine our success:

- The **clinical** arena: how we feel, think, and behave;

- The **relational** arena: how we relate to others; and

- The **performance** arena: how we perform and what we achieve.

Siegel, who has studied the formation of the brain and mind in the context of relationships, sums up their curative power better than anyone I know. He pulls all of the research together with a threefold focus, which he refers to as the **triangle** of well-being, in his *Pocket Guide to Interpersonal Neurobiology: An Integrative Handbook of the Mind* (New York: Norton, 2012).

This triangle of well-being determines how we do in the areas of life that matter to us daily—whether or not the Navy SEAL finishes the swim, whether or not a marriage is enriching and happy, whether or not the CEO is able to lead a team, whether or not a child develops intellectually, whether or not you are able to fight off adversity and be resilient. The three elements that form the triangle of well-being work together to build, drive, create, and regulate our functioning and performance. What are the three? They are our brain/body (the physical), our relational connections, and our minds, which regulate the energy and information needed to live and perform.

Siegel describes the triangle as a "process . . . that regulates the flow of energy and information within our social interactions and our neural firing patterns . . . it is not brain *or* relationships . . . it is a system that entails the flow of energy and information **within the brain and between one another.**" Our brain works in the context of relationships, and develops a *regulating mind* that controls the flow of our energy and the information that drives everything. We are connected in such ways that the reality of how we function always involves these three elements: *our physical makeup, our relationships, and our minds.*

Siegel continues: "Just as a coin has a heads, tails, and edge, the one reality of energy and information flow has at least three facets: sharing in '**relationships,**' embodied mechanism in '**brain,**' and regulation in '**mind.**'" We need *all* three elements, all three parts of the triangle, **to produce change and high performance.** When we strengthen each side of the triangle, our well-being increases. And that only happens because of, and through, relationships. Said another way, for us to get to the next level, we need relationships that help us develop both our brains and our minds in very specific ways. When those relationships operate in a certain way, we get better. When they don't, we don't. We either stay the same or go backward.

Since that wake-up moment for me in college, calling me to find out that it was the *quality of relationships* that matters, I've seen firsthand that helping people enhance performance and grow past limits involves a *lot* more than merely hanging out. Well-being *depends* on being in relationships, but clearly in very specific ways, imparting very specific information and coding through relational interactions, energy flow, and regulation—all of which build performance capacity in the mind, brain, and body. It's not about relationships *or* information; it's about both. But it's also about certain *experiences* in our relationships that cause our very mental and physical equipment to grow, develop to a higher level, and perform better than it could before. It takes relationship, *but of a certain kind.* That is what gets us to the next level, and that is the subject of this book.

The triangle of well-being must be constructed in a particular way, so that relationships, brain, and mind all work together to *grow our abilities past current limits.* The dynamics of the relationship must be ordered in a certain way and infused with certain kinds of information, coding, or patterning. Just as a computer has specific code that runs its operating system, so do the "codes" embedded in relationships get internalized over time. Our relationships help write the "code" of whom we become and are becoming. Relationships have power, for good and for bad. Good and bad "code," and good and bad "energy." They affect all three parts of the triangle of well-being: the physical, the interpersonal, and the psychological.

Let's look at each of these three parts and why they are all important in our functioning.

First, there is the **brain** and the nervous system considered as a whole, the physical organ that embodies all of these processes, drives them, and is affected by them. How we perform, relate, achieve, feel, and behave is dramatically affected by what is happening in our physical brains. Our brains run on electrical charges and chemicals, such as neurotransmitters and hormones. Its nerve cells and their interactions comprise all of the physical equipment that Siegel refers to as the "neural firing." Think of how the circuitry in a computer—the motherboard, the microchip, the electrical wiring, the battery—affects its performance; similarly, the wiring of our brains fundamentally affects how well we do.

Take an easy illustration. When your hormones change, your behavior changes, how you feel changes, how you relate to others changes. If your serotonin gets depleted, your mood changes, as well as your ability to concentrate and focus. Your energy drops. Insulin functioning changes your glucose levels; then your thinking, energy, behavior, and a host of other performance drivers are affected as well. That's why athletes refuel themselves. The brain, the physical equipment, is a huge part of all of our functioning. But it's not *all* there is.

Second, there is **relationship**, our interpersonal connections and our experiences in those connections. By relationship we are talking not just about hanging out with your pals in a fraternity house. We are talking about *specific qualitative relational connectedness*. Neuroscience has shown us that these kinds of relationships, even seemingly insignificant ones, greatly enhance performance and even help build, fuel, and sustain the physical connections hardwired in the brain.

This is why you can feel very differently and perform very differently, depending on whom you are with and what is going on in that relationship. Moreover, *it is in relationships that our minds are actually built*. These relationships affect not only our bodies and brains, but our mind's abilities as well. Infants who have a loving, caring, supportive, and attuned relationship develop all sorts of internal physical and mental equipment thereby.

The neural equipment that results from those relationships will enable them to connect with others, empathize with others, and develop intellectually and physically. Healthy relationship wires their brains for a host of functions—such as the ability to regulate their own emotions, solve problems, deal with stress, and be resilient. As we shall see, business leaders, athletes, and other high performers build their equipment through relationships utilizing the very same mechanisms.

The structure, activities, and quality of those relationships are crucial. If the relationships are positive, attuned, empathic, caring, supportive, and challenging, then they cause positive development in the brain and increase performance capacities. If they are not quality connections, they either cause *nothing* to happen when something *should* be happening, or *bad* things to be built into us when they *shouldn't* be—"bugs," such as an overreactive brain, distrust, squirrelly thinking, an inability to focus and attend, impulsivity, controlling behavior, sensitivity to failure, and other liabilities that interfere with our performance.

Third, there's the **mind**—and this is the biggest reason I believe my professor was wrong in implying therapy was *only* about relationship. The mind is the psychological equipment that regulates it all, the essential software process that keeps it all flowing and working to win . . . or not. As Siegel describes it, the mind "regulates the flow of energy and information within our bodies and within our relationships, an emergent and self-organizing process that gives rise to our mental activities such as emotion, thinking, and memory." Our minds process all that is going on at any moment, enabling us to do well or not.

This is why we can't just be "in a relationship," or just have a "friend" and expect that to do all that we need to get to the next level. Just anyone won't do. There is the building of real *equipment* inside, the building of our *minds* that regulate life and our function-ing. The mind, or mental process, must be developed to regulate the flow of energy and information within our bodies and within our relationships to engage the outside world of all performance. This development gives rise to the ability to think differently, feel differ-ently, regulate ourselves differently, and perform better. We must not only focus on relationships, but also on building the equipment in our minds, which will drive the performance. It's an important distinction that I'll reiterate throughout this book. Yes, relationship matters, but it must be the *kind* of relationship that builds good equipment—the technology of your mind, if you will—to improve performance.

Better performance comes from enhancing the equipment—in computer parlance, the processor and the software—that drives the performance. It's about increasing the horsepower of your performance "engine" and your ability to regulate yourself. Such improvements are built through certain kinds of relational experi-ences, energy, and information working together as you experience growth. Your body/brain, relational experience, and your mind work together to make it all work . . . or not. Relationships, the "power of the other," cannot be neglected in the formula of get-ting to your next level. They are central to it all. The physical, the relational, and the mental, all working together but truly built in relationship.

My goal here is to help you see that the things we always try to do to get better—which includes working on our abilities, thinking styles, initiative, strategy, communication, accountability, persever-ance, adaptability, and so forth—are certainly valid, but insuffi-cient. The problem is that you can't just change them on your own.

You are already at your limits with the equipment you have. But your abilities will be changed, and your equipment will grow, as these capacities are developed in certain kinds of relationships.

To get to the next level of performance, you certainly do have to think differently, but to think differently, you have to have a different mind, and your brain has to fire differently. To develop these differences in your mind and brain, the equipment in which thoughts and feelings and behaviors are embodied, you need to connect in ways that rewire you.

CHANGE DEMYSTIFIED

I was meeting with a CEO of a nationwide company to review our coaching sessions after a year and a half of working together. "It's interesting," he commented. "I'm struck by the differences now. I can't believe how *differently I'm thinking in the business* and the growth that is coming because of it. Professionally and personally, I'm in a different place than I was when we started out—a place I couldn't even see back then. But there is a mystery to it . . . something I don't understand."

"What is it?" I asked.

"Well, you question my thinking a lot. But, it's not like you tell me *what* to think or what to do, specifically, very often. In fact, sometimes I've wished for more structured to-do lists when I leave here. I want you to tell me sometimes to 'go do these things.' I want to be able to push the process even further, faster, so that I can keep getting better."

I started laughing . . . out loud. He looked at me and asked, "Why are you laughing? What did I say?"

So I told him. "What I am laughing at is the way that growth, getting to the next level, works—it's not something we can control, or will into being, or just choose . . . even though you would like to be able to do that, right? We both know you like to control things. But getting better is not about just 'willing' better performance. *It's about becoming someone who performs better, and performs differently. It's about changing the equipment.*"

He did see the humor. He had been growing as the result of a process, not by willpower or by working through a big to-do list each time. Certainly he had been working on specific things I had given him to do, even many assignments. But the change he was seeing in his performance really was more outside of his control than he would have liked it to be. Like a lot of top leaders, he had a real love of being in control and structuring things. But getting better is not a solo act and not something that you can control. His growth had been in using our relationship and in ordering other relationships in his work that would have the result of his becoming different and thereby performing differently. His equipment was changing.

"It's the process," I said. "Just do what you've been doing. . . . We'll keep working on the things you bring in, and you'll go back out and work them through in the ways we discuss, and you will continue to change. . . . You will think differently because your 'thinker' is changing. It's getting more horsepower. Trust it. It works."

He then confirmed my statement with an example. He recounted how, in a recent board meeting, he'd been drilled by the chairman about the terms of a deal he had just taken the company through. The chairman wondered aloud whether the CEO had effectively protected the company from a competitor in the structuring of the deal. It sounded as though the chairman was questioning whether the CEO really had a plan for the future and whether or not he was anticipating how to defend the company against the competitor as they moved against them.

"In the past, I would have immediately been thinking about the defensive moves we'd have to take to protect ourselves and to show him that I was going to play good defense against the competitor. But this time I was different. For some reason, I was really calm and told him, 'Not only is it not a problem, but I have taken steps to make sure that we've made it more than hard for our competitors to catch up.' I then outlined the *offensive* strategy that I had put into place that would totally make the competitor have to exit the landscape. I basically was not thinking of playing defense at all. I was thinking very different thoughts, thoughts about *offense*. I had put us in a completely different position in the market than I would have before . . . by moving from just defense to playing offense. Those are truly different thoughts—and I wasn't *telling* myself to do that; it was just happening. And I find that it keeps happening. I'm thinking different thoughts."

"Those capacities will only increase," I reassured him, "as you continue to grow. You're not going to have to 'will yourself' to perform better. You're just going to perform better because your equipment is different. It will act differently."

POWERFUL FINDINGS

Imagine not trying to *control* your reactions or feelings of stress, but actually not reacting, actually not feeling stressed by what stresses you now. Imagine not trying to change or control what you are about to say to someone, but actually having different responses come out of your mouth without having to bite your tongue on the old ones. That is what real growth is about—qualitative differences in our performance equipment, which spits out different performance. You will discover that that kind of growth happens in key relationships with key dynamics, and as they are present, you will grow, change, and increase your capacity. That is the result of the power of the other.

How powerful are the effects of relationship done in certain ways? Here are just a few of the variables on which relational connections produce qualitative and quantitative effects:

- How long you live

- Whether you reach or don't reach your goals

- Whether or not you close the sale

- How much money you make

- How well your kids do in school

- How much you trust people

- How you cope with stress and failure

- What kind of mood you're in

- How much physical pain you experience

- How and what you think

Think about some of these variables and how we normally approach them. If, for example, you want to live longer, do you tend to focus more on what you eat and how much you exercise and whether or not you smoke? Do you focus on counting fats, calories, and push-ups? *Or do you also focus on whether or not you are connecting with people you are close to and sharing your life with them?*

If you are trying to reach a goal, do you focus only on your strategy, or on *whom you are going to engage to help you get there?*

If you are trying to change a behavior, do you set out a target for change, and begin to try to live up to that target? *Or do you seek coaching and support that will help you get there?*

If you are trying to build a successful business or grow the one you have, do you focus on strategy and execution only? *Or do you focus on building a thriving culture?*

When you try to close a sale or get an investor to back your venture, do you focus on the rational reason to buy in? *Or do you focus on the relationship and shared values?*

Whatever we hope to achieve, our success depends on relationships with others. Without the help of others or with negative dynamics from destructive others, we will usually fail. There is no standing still. We are either thriving in relational energy and growth or we are going backward, slowly or quickly.

In the rest of this book, we will look at the effects of specific kinds of relationships and how they help or hinder us in getting past whatever our current limit might be.

- How we are *always* seeking connection, sometimes to not-so-good ends, and what to do about that reality

- How our own stance in our relationships determines whether or not those relationships will be helpful to us

- How we are fueled for greater performance

- How we gain self-control and mastery for performance

- How ownership that drives performance is built through relationship

- How we overcome the adversarial nature of standards that makes us resist our goals

- The role of structure and time in developing capacity and horsepower

- The most destructive dynamic in relational systems

- How trust is built and maintained in capacity-building relationships

I have chosen these areas for a few reasons. First of all, they represent many of the major dynamics involved in creating high performance. As you will see, each one is an important building block to get to the next level, no matter where you or your team might find yourselves. These issues include fueling, self-mastery, ownership, goal acceleration, structure, and others. Second, the truth is that each of these dynamics requires relationship in order to increase capacity. They all are grown in the triangle that we've just discussed. And we will examine the nature of the relationships that will make that triangle thrive.

Let's get started by asking the first and most important question: "Where are you?"

CHAPTER THREE

THE FOUR CORNERS
OF CONNECTION

Your plane lands, and the flight attendant says, "It is now safe to use your mobile phones." You turn yours on, and what's the first thing that happens? You receive a message at the top of the screen that reads: "Searching . . ." or "Searching for connection . . ." or "Searching for network . . ."

Until the phone connects with the network, nothing happens. But when it connects, miracles occur, in the invisible world. The phone's capabilities are now empowered to be all they were designed to be. It can now automatically download or fix bugs in the software; it can download new apps that enable it to do things it couldn't do before. Through this connection, all of the resources of the outside world are suddenly at your disposal and ready to provide benefit. Through this link, the phone connects you to the entire world, all of its information and knowledge, help and skill, to enable better performance. From this one connection, almost anything is possible. The phone surpasses its previous limits . . . it can get bigger, and better.

But without a connection to the right network, that little device will never be able to do everything it was designed to do. Sure, it might still be able to tell you the time or see a calendar of your events or serve as a repository of previous communication and photos, but without a strong and steady connection, nothing *new* or *better* can occur. Without a connection, the device has hit its limit. It continues to produce the same results you were producing on the plane, even if you try harder.

Humans are exactly like that. You are like that; I am like that. From the moment we are born, the moment we land, a "chip" inside each of us starts searching for a connection to the right network, one that will provide us with the energy and information (coding) to go beyond our present ability, experience, and performance. And this searching, this needing a connection, is not optional for any of us. It is hardwired and always on, even when we don't know it and even when we don't even desire it.

As long as you are alive, your heart and mind and soul will be searching for a connection. An "other." Several others. A community that will bring life, all the ingredients of life that you need to get past the limit of your present existence and performance.

The need for connection begins before infancy and continues throughout life—from the womb to the tomb. If you are alive, you need it to thrive, period.

We are fueled from the outside, from connection with others. Whether it's a smartphone or a human, when the system can't make a connection, it begins to run down. This is an indisputable reality. Humans need connection, and their systems are always searching for one.

A FAILURE TO THRIVE

When I explained this process to a board chairman recently, he replied, "You've just explained our last three years and the reason we had to fire our CEO."

"How's that?" I asked.

"We had a superstar," he said. "Or at least we thought so. He was so smart and talented . . . had it all. But slowly we began to see that something wasn't right. The culture of the company was changing under him—less energy, less teamwork, less passion. And the direction began to get fuzzy."

Then it got worse. The chairman went on to explain that the CEO was like an island. Even though he would be "out there" making presentations and interacting around the company, no one really felt that they could get close to him. When the board would try to give input, he'd often just shut down and close himself off. His executive team felt that he really wasn't part of his own team. He didn't engage with them or seek their input much at all.

Then it started to affect his decision making. He moved further afield from the goals the team and the board had set and started pursuing his own private agenda—without any input. He ended up costing the company a lot of time and money to mend fences and get out of shaky deals. It was clear the CEO had to go.

"The funny thing is that until now," the chairman continued, shaking his head, "I never realized that the main problem was not his decisions or the strategy he wanted to pursue, but the fact that he was so disconnected—from the board, his own team, and really the organization. His decisions were coming out of his disconnectedness."

A cell phone may look as though it's working . . . for a while. It can compute things, run programs, and maintain basic functioning, but if it doesn't find a connection—and the right one and soon—it won't be of much use. That's the dynamic that exists in human performance as well.

WHERE ARE YOU?

Have you ever gone into a restaurant to meet a friend, sat down, and heard them ask, "So, where are you?"

Funny question, if you think about it. You could say, "I am sitting right here, you idiot. Where do you think I am?"

But you know that's not what they are really asking you. They are asking something much more profound: "Where are *you*. . . . the real you? Your heart, mind, and soul? The internal you?" They are asking "How are you doing? How is your existence?"

It's interesting that we use the word *where* in that context, as if we're talking about a literal place, some sort of interior space. And no wonder: you *are* "somewhere"—in a good place or a bad place.

That somewhere is a state of *connectedness*, even when you are by yourself, so the next time someone asks, "Where are you?" give it more serious thought. The ability to answer that question can change everything about your performance, your growth—and your life.

THE POSSIBILITIES OF WHERE
YOU ARE

The reality is that you are always in one of *four* places of connection. No matter what life circumstances you are going through on the outside—victory or defeat, or somewhere in between—there are only *four possibilities of connection* that you can be in at any given time. It is the premise of this book, and science and experience agree, that figuring out *where you are* is one of the most important things you can do for yourself.

While there are four different kinds of connectedness—four possible corners of our relational space—only one of them will help you thrive. The other three corners will always diminish your performance and your well-being. They can even destroy your vision, your relationships, your performance, and your health. The key is to get out of any of the other three and into the only one that works. Think of this dynamic as the geography of relationships, a map with four corners:

1. Disconnected, No Connection

2. The Bad Connection

3. The Pseudo-Good Connection

4. True Connection

CORNER NUMBER ONE:
DISCONNECTED

The CEO described earlier in this chapter is the perfect example of someone living in Corner One. Sometimes a person can be extroverted, even always around others, but *still* be disconnected. In fact, some of the most disconnected people on the earth, sociopaths and some narcissists, can be very charming and lure others in at first. But they aren't able to make a real emotional investment in others. True connection always means being emotionally and functionally invested in other people, in a give-and-receive dynamic. Disconnection lacks something, in one direction or the other—either in the giving or the receiving. Truly connected people do both. They are emotionally present and able to give and to receive.

As leaders, people residing in Corner One tend not to build strong relational cultures. The culture might be high-performance and demanding, but people don't feel that their contributions are valued or that they are truly cared about. And even though there might be good business results, these are usually short-lived, and then the lack of deep, positive relationships and a caring culture begins to erode trust and goodwill. It goes more and more toxic. The healthiest and most talented people usually leave to work at places where they'll feel more valued, where they can be part of something with a soul.

Under disconnected leaders, decision making tends to be done in isolation, either solely by the leaders or in organizational silos that they build or foster. Sometimes disconnected leaders allow one or two people into their worlds, but usually only to act as human shields, allowing the Corner One leader to stay in a bubble. Such a shield might be a colleague, a direct report, a spouse, or anyone else who helps the leader stay disconnected from the whole, and that connection itself is usually not very healthy—mutually beneficial, they both may feel, but not healthy.

This model of "closed system" leadership does exactly what all closed systems do: it gets worse over time. Without taking in outside energy and intelligence, decisions get goofier and goofier, cut off from some key realities or stakeholders. Key people and other stakeholders begin to wonder, "What was he thinking? He's so out of touch."

Leaders operating from Corner One are frustrating and confusing to be around, so imagine what it's like to be in a *personal* relationship with a disconnected person. It is even worse than a professional one. It can be a lonely place . . . a strange, sometimes crazy-making experience.

Interactions that should be fulfilling leave the partner feeling unheard, misunderstood, unable to have any impact on the disconnected party, who lacks empathy or expresses it only superficially and is unable to truly be supportive of others. In fact, sometimes those in Corner One treat others as if they have no feelings, seeming to have no awareness of the other people at all. If you are in a relationship like that you might feel like musician George Thorogood when he sings, "When I drink alone, I prefer to be by myself."

Over time, those in a relationship with a disconnected person tend to lose heart and withdraw. We have all experienced, somewhere in life, being in some sort of significant relationship that was supposed to offer connection but didn't. Even then, though, the search for real connection continues.

STUCK IN CORNER ONE

So far I've described what it's like to try to connect to someone in Corner One. It's tough, it's lonely, and it's not sustainable. But what if I've just described you—stuck in Corner One—even if you weren't previously aware of it? If you want to find out where you are, just ask the people in your life who depend on you. Ask them if they feel needed, valued, listened to, and taken into your confidence. If they answer yes, then you are probably not stuck in Corner One. Indeed, if you are reading this and understanding it, then you are unlikely to be living in Corner One.

But even if you're not totally cut off, it's still possible that your connections aren't as strong as they should be or as healthy as you want them to be, and that you do have some Corner One realities going on. This is very common for high performers.

For whatever reasons, life has taught you that you have to do things on your own. In very practical ways, you do not allow yourself to need anyone. And although you care about others and give to *them*, you are disconnected from your own needs. You are giving—sometimes a lot—but you are not taking much in. It's easy for you to help others but difficult for you to allow them to help you, especially emotionally.

Sometimes this is even the natural path by which someone gets into leadership: a kid is a doer, the family hero, or a caretaker—the one everyone else depends on. I can't tell you how many CEOs I have worked with who were the higher-performing sibling who learned early to make up for what others weren't doing. Early in life, they became the persons others depended on, not the ones who

depended upon others. But when they continue that style of interaction in the executive suite, in a marriage, or in other significant
relationships that must thrive on mutual interdependency, it creates
problems for them. They are always putting out, performing for
others, getting it done, and yet rarely ever taking in what they need
from the outside world.

Worse than that, leadership roles can drive someone into
Corner One. How many times have we heard that it's lonely at the
top? Many leaders do feel alone, but it doesn't have to be that way,
and the best leaders create conditions that help them avoid being
pulled into Corner One. Certainly some aspects of leadership require making tough decisions, being the one who owns it, the place
where the buck stops. But leadership isn't supposed to be lonely or
isolated. When it is, something is wrong, and it can be fixed.

Recently a CEO called me while she was going through some
extreme difficulties—more than most leaders ever have to deal
with. I asked what her board was saying to her.

"What?" she replied. "I haven't told them about any of this."

"Why not?" I asked. I knew of the board's affection and respect
for her, but even more important, I was aware of the strengths, net-
works, and advice they would have been able to offer her.

"I can't let them see me in this kind of vulnerable state. I can't
reach out to them like this," she said.

"Again, why not?" I pressed.

"Because they all look to me to be the leader," she said. "They
look to me to make it all work, which I know I can do. But I can't
let them know how much I'm having a difficult time."

"Are you kidding me?" I said. "If you can't, then they're not
a board. They should all be fired. If their CEO is going through

something, they of all people should know it and be there for you in this. I know they will. They don't look to you to be Super-woman . . . they look to you to be a CEO. And you're doing a great job, and will continue to. But in this season, this is where you need their help and support. And you especially need that in order to keep doing a great job! This is part of their oversight."

I finally got through to her, and she did let them in on what was going on. And that one step changed everything. They rallied to her side and got her out of the deadly Corner Number One.

Nevertheless, as we all know, sometimes it is wise, appropriate, and strategic not to lay all your cards on the table. It goes without saying that the workplace can be a highly competitive arena where people operate with self-interest and mixed motives. But that's all the more reason to find someplace where you can get the connec-tions we all seek.

If you can't find connection in one aspect of your life, even if only temporarily, then all the more reason to seek it in other sup-portive relationships. If you find yourself in a situation where there is absolutely *nowhere* you can be vulnerable, nowhere you can con-nect to a network of people for energy, support, downloads, and the like, then something is really wrong. Leadership, shame, fear, pressure, or habit has pushed you into a corner in which you cannot thrive and may ultimately fail.

I was in an editorial meeting during the writing of this book, and one person said, "Oh, I remember having that boss. I could not be real with him . . . too dangerous. But I knew that surviving him meant that my best friend at work and I had to do regular huddles to support each other and remind each other that it was him who was crazy and not us! It would help us before and after we had to talk to him." Perfect. Even with impossible people, you can't let them turn you into someone who is not opening up to anyone at all, and winding up in Corner One. But it happens too often.

Bill Hybels, founder of the Global Leadership Summit, and I conducted a leadership retreat for several years where we would bring in a group of high-performing leaders from both the business and the nonprofit world for a couple of days of leadership coaching on Lake Michigan. It was a great time for leaders to get away, be with peers, and think about various areas of their leadership.

Soon I began giving participants a questionnaire to gather data on how their leadership worlds functioned. A few of the questions were geared specifically toward finding out how much just being in their leadership role had forced them into an isolated Corner Number One. Here's some of what I found:

- **Question One:** Do you have someplace where you can be 100 percent honest and vulnerable as to what you are going through in your leadership role, where you can totally be honest about struggles, conflicts, needs, weaknesses, etc.?

- **Results:** 80 percent of leaders said "No. I have no place like that."

- **Question Two:** Do you have anyone or any group of people who is totally committed to your growth and well-being as a leader? The very role of that relationship is just to develop and help you?

- **Results:** 80 percent of leaders said "No. I have no place like that."

And now the kicker:

- **Question:** Have you experienced anything in the last year that you would say has gotten to "clinical proportions?" Burnout, loss of energy, difficulty getting motivated, concentration or focus problems, anxiety or stress, depression, an addiction or other habit, sleep problems, etc.

- **Results:** 80 percent of leaders said "Yes."

Life and leadership in Corner Number One has its costs.

Corner Number One, the corner of disconnection, does *not* mean that you might not be a people person. Nor does it necessarily mean that you don't have people in your life or that you might not be helping a lot of others. Lots of people in Corner One seem to be people persons, constantly helping others. It *does* mean that it's all coming from you. You might be giving to others and having a lot of others around you, but you are not connecting to them so that anyone is there for you, in the deepest ways that you need them. This is a recipe for burnout and diminished or limited performance at best, and failing or derailing at worst.

Do you want to know how you're doing if you're in Corner Number One? Here are the signs to look out for:

- **Clinical:** Increased stress; lower energy levels, concentration, and motivation; problems sleeping; lowered libido; increased fear and anxiety; increased levels of suspicion, distrust, and resentment; loss of hope and purpose.

- **Relational**: Not feeling as connected to others as you once did—even at home and in your personal life, more isolation, detachment from those you care most about, conflicts with those you're close to, shortness of temper, lack of patience, anger, or just not wanting to be involved or around others. Loss of interest in relationship, in being with people. Disappointment with relationship itself, and a feeling of just being cut off.

- **Performance**: Not getting the results you need and feeling as if it all depends upon you to do so; not being able to get "on top of it all," procrastination, disorganization, lack of clarity about goals, feeling bogged down by tasks someone else should be doing, diminished focus.

Does any of this sound familiar? Doesn't sound like much fun, does it?

CORNER NUMBER TWO: A BAD CONNECTION

We are made for connection, remember? The "chip" inside is always searching, even if we're sometimes afraid or unaware of it. At some point, for most people, Corner One gives way to Corner Number Two: *the Bad Connection*. It is as if the connecting chip makes a calculation that a bad relationship is better than no relationship at all. It's not a conscious move, mind you. I mean, who would actively seek out a bad connection? But it seems to happen more than any of us want to admit.

Corner Number Two, the Bad Connection, is not necessarily a connection with a bad or abusive person, although it may be. Instead, *it is a connection, preoccupation, or pull toward a person who has the effect of making you feel bad or "not good enough" in some way.* Inferior. Defective perhaps. As though something is wrong with you. Somehow this person or persons have come to have the power in your life of making you feel bad.

It could be a boss, a board member, a customer, a friend, a family member, or a direct report. They come in all sizes and shapes and affiliations. But the one common ingredient is that *they have the power to make you feel bad.* High expectations, perfectionism, unreasonable demands, a critical spirit, withholding of praise, shame, guilt, put-downs, silence—these are just a few of the many ways that a person like this can hook someone into feeling the Corner Number Two bad connection.

What happens then? Your leadership, energy, well-being, focus, and passion get diverted and diminished. You start playing defense, trying to catch up. You try to get back to even, to a place where the other person will feel good about you again and you can feel good about yourself, so you spend inordinate amounts of time worrying about being good enough in that person's eyes. I recently heard a leader prepare a report for his critical CEO and comment, "This might even get a good reaction out of *her.*" He was always trying to get to neutral or positive with her, as he always felt not good enough for her.

I told him, "Give it up. She doesn't give good reactions. As long as you're looking for that from her, you will be miserable."

The experience of being in Corner Two is a universal human experience. Still, I have been amazed by the number of extremely high performers, some admired all over the world, who have confided to me that someone has that power to make them feel not good enough—from sports to business to entertainment, literal superstars who cannot shake the feeling of disapproval and disappointment from that particular someone.

Perhaps you have been in this corner in your own life. Things might be going well, or you might be in a tough season. It doesn't really matter. It has more to do with what that particular person thinks of you than how things are objectively going. It is about their disapproval or criticism or lack of support for something not being as they think it should be—not helpful criticism, but rather a critical tone, spirit, and connection.

No matter what else is going on, if you are in Corner Two, for some reason the chip inside of you has connected to *this particular network*, a critical one in several senses of the word, this connection with a person who makes you feel bad about yourself, or your work, or your life. The connection produces anxiety, fear, guilt, shame, and feelings of badness or inferiority. It causes sleepless nights obsessing over what this person or group thinks of you, replaying what you did wrong or could have done better. And so on.

Besides making you feel bad, probably the worst effect of Corner Number Two is what it does to your performance and your functioning. No one delivers a great performance while lost in negative self-evaluation. Corner Number Two annihilates high performance through self-doubt and self-deprecation. You become more concerned with gaining someone's approval than with the performance itself. Simply stated, when that is happening, you have become *less of you*. Trying to measure up, trying to get some-one to approve—that's playing defense in its most crippling form. You should be playing and concentrating on the game, but instead you're concentrating on what someone else thinks about how you are playing. You can't have divided focus and your best perfor-mance at the same time. Impossible.

For Kevin, the bad connection was his new boss. Kevin had done well in his position as president of the company for several years. All of the performance indicators were up. The board liked him. He was having the time of his life . . . until he wasn't.

The CEO of the holding company, to whom he reported, retired, and the board put a new one in place. From the outset, Kevin was not the new guy's favorite. For unknown reasons, the new CEO just didn't seem to share the same feelings that others had about Kevin and his performance. It was as if he were wired differently, and no matter how Kevin tried to work with him, the relationship never really took off. Most of the CEO's interactions with Kevin involved his not liking something or wanting things done differently. It was not all negative, but certainly lukewarm on the best days and virtually never encouraging.

Slowly this great performer was being diminished by the withholding CEO. Kevin would think about it a lot, asking him-self repeatedly what he could do to make it better. Every time he thought he'd done something that would please the new CEO, he'd be disappointed in the response he would get. That is when the spiral began.

Kevin, now playing defense, was no longer being *all* of himself. He had moved into response reactive mode. He started second-guessing himself and worrying about each and every action he took. In a word, he'd lost his mojo—the edge that great leaders have. Life in Corner Number Two, feeling inferior to someone's appraisal of him, was taking its toll.

Sometimes you don't even need another person to experience this not-being-good-enough feeling. You might be having a primary connection not with someone like Kevin's boss, but with your own *internal* critical voices. It doesn't even take a boss or another person to drive you into Corner Two; you end up there all by yourself. You can even do it in your car driving alone!

That happens when your primary connection is with an internal judge who has lived inside your head for a long time—perhaps someone from your formative years or a significant other from your past. The message implanted by that person becomes the one your chip seems to always connect to, getting a response that leaves you feeling not good enough, playing defense. By comparing yourself to some unrealistic, nonexistent standard, you're always failing.

No matter whether a move into Corner Two is triggered by a real person or by voices in your head, your performance suffers. You begin to take failure personally. Any bad event or result becomes proof that you are not good enough. As your confidence wanes, you find yourself smack-dab in Corner Two.

WHAT CORNER TWO LOOKS LIKE

If you've ever seen a good boxing match, you know there's a moment that everyone recognizes as the turning point. It happens in other sports as well, but you can see it especially well in boxing. It's that moment when one fighter is back on his or her heels, fending off blows rather than delivering them, no longer in control.

The sight of a person, especially a leader, focused on getting someone's approval, on performing better in order to be good enough or to "make it" in some way, has the same look and feel. Other people recognize that you are back on your heels, taking punches instead of throwing them.

Team members, especially executive team members, lose respect with this kind of leader and eventually lose heart. Over the years, I've had many conversations with team members who've expressed these sentiments about their leader. "I wish he would just stop wanting people to like him, and just take charge. It seems like a few other people around here have somehow usurped his authority, or at least his influence. They have more power than he does . . . even though he has the leadership position. We need him to step up and lead."

Leaders playing defense are often in approval-seeking mode, even as they mount a new campaign or introduce a new product or strategy. *There is more attempt at selling it than declaring it.* True performance is an expression, not a request to be liked or praised. Usually, when someone needs approval, there's less to approve of.

CORNER NUMBER THREE: THE SEDUCTIVELY FALSE "GOOD CONNECTION"

Let's face it. No one wants to feel isolated, alone, or inadequate. Those are all pretty unpleasant feelings, so at some point, your connection-seeking chip is going to say, "Enough of this. I want to feel *good*." So it finds something to connect to that feels good.

Whereas a Corner Two connection leaves you feeling bad, or not good enough in some way, in Corner Three it's the opposite. You feel good! Sometimes really good. The positive feelings take a variety of forms: the affair, the addiction, the attachment to promotions, awards, or positive results, the next acquisition, the next big product launch, accolades from others. Food, sex, drugs, . . . a new Ferrari. It's all an attempt to soothe the soul. The problem is that painkillers do not really cure the disease. They just ease the pain, temporarily and superficially making one feel better.

I have seen leaders addicted to good news. They want to hear only about what is going well. It feels good. They want to be surrounded by employees and board members who tell them they're great and their ideas are stellar. They love the idolizing fans, the status of their position, the accolades, the private jets, and all the other perks.

When I was working with one Corner Three CEO, I saw the phenomenon more than once. Each time he was confronted with a failure or a setback, he would soon come up with a glitzy new strategy or campaign that would capture his energy. The next shiny object. It would get him all excited so that he would be over the last letdown. Once his board started to recognize the pattern, they had to stop him from venturing into another launch of bliss, but until then, his Corner Three escapades cost them plenty.

For Jeremy, it was his chief of staff who thought he could do no wrong. She was always there to stand in the gap with him, comfort him, and agree with his decisions and his evaluation of the people above him who had gotten it wrong. If things failed, she reassured him that it wasn't his fault. Blame the big bosses, the economy, the industry, the regulators—whatever, as long as it soothed his feelings of defeat. And when things went well, she was there to make him feel like the star that he wanted to be.

She pumped him up and made him feel better, made him feel "good." This connection shielded him against the things that were not going well all around him. The problem was that like all Corner Three connections, it wasn't real. It was flattery. Things were actually not as good as she professed. She was medicating him against reality.

Flattery is perhaps the worst drug of all for Corner Three leaders. They thrive on it, and unfortunately their position puts them in the exactly right circumstance for the pushers of this drug. They have the title that makes them feel that the flattery actually means something about them, when in reality they are being controlled and manipulated by the flatterer. Many people think their way up the ladder of success is to flatter their leaders. While this is a death trap for both, for the leader it is often a drug with an extra-strong appeal, and an extra-strong diminishing effect: it actually makes the leader dependent on the people he or she is leading. He "needs" that flattery to feel good, and at that point, it gets confusing as to "who's the tick and who's the dog." The Corner Three person needs more and more, as it's never enough.

Substances, awards, accolades, the approval of yes-men and sycophants, sexual acting out, indulgence in hobbies or materialism—they all have the power to make us feel good . . . for a minute. Then, we need another fix. Another good report. Another record quarter or sales number. The old problems remain, and we need one more dose. It never can really do the trick.

Like all forms of addiction, the drive for more itself becomes the reason for being. Every day is a striving to find one more good feeling about oneself or within oneself.

WHAT CORNER THREE LOOKS LIKE

Corners One and Two are downers, but Corner Three lets the good times roll. It's fun. High energy. Electric at times. The person or leader who is experiencing Corner Three is on an endorphin high. Champagne is flowing; high fives rule the day. Sometimes entire companies can get caught up in the hype. Even Enron looked good for a moment. And a flattering affair can certainly feel good . . . for a while.

I have run across many executive teams who wish their CEO would turn around from facing the outside world and look at them, connect with them, be involved with them and what they have going, instead of flitting around the country or the world hanging out with "important people" and attending events that "make him feel cool." Certainly part of a leader's role is to be a public spokesperson and a corporate diplomat. But that's not what I'm talking about.

There are certain leaders who begin to give their teams the impression that being a celebrity, or at least hanging out with celebrities, is more important than their teams and the real work. The feeling that it's all about the leader doesn't wear well. The feeling that their leader doesn't want to hear any bad news doesn't wear well. The leader—or the spouse, for that matter—who doesn't want to hear any criticism or disagreement with his or her ideas loses respect after a while. The connection runs shallow, and the shielded one looks out of touch, shallow, and self-centered.

There are a thousand ways we humans have come up with to self-medicate, but they are all ultimately a trap of our own devising and lead to diminishing performance. One executive I worked with figured out that her Corner Three was retail therapy. When I explained the concept of Four Corners to her, she gave me a stunned look. She led me to a storage room in her office and showed me the evidence: dresses, shoes, clothes, accessories, all purchased at work. When I asked her about it, she said, "I see it now. It's a Corner Number Three. When things are not going well, or I have a tough interaction with one of my bosses, I take a break. I slip out and go shopping. Until now, I just thought it was a normal break and getting away from it all. Now I can see . . . it's medicine. It's a connection. It's . . . she stalled for a minute . . . a relationship. I have a connection with retail!"

Another leader was addicted to Fantasy Football. All he needed was a little stress, something to make him feel a little down, and he could lose hours on his computer. Any golfers, hunters, fishermen, or web surfing sports enthusiasts listening?

Another CEO I work with was late for a dinner meeting. When he arrived, he said, "I have a confession."

"What?" I asked.

"I have a sexual addiction . . . mostly internet porn. And I have been seeking some help for it in a recovery group. And that is why I am late," he said.

"What happened?" I inquired.

"Well, I have learned something. One of my triggers is when an authority figure, like a boss or important customer, criticizes me. I run to my addiction for comfort. It makes me feel better.

"On the way here, I had to call my sponsor and process how I was doing. My boss was pretty down on me today, and when I left the office, I felt tempted to go do something that would make me feel good, but that I would regret. So I called my sponsor and we talked for a while, until it all passed. That's why I'm late, and as part of my recovery, I had to be honest about it and tell you," he said.

What he had learned was that Corner Three had been a place of comfort for him. It made him feel good when other things were not feeling so great. But it wouldn't last, and it also was undermining his marriage and other aspects of his life.

Sex, food, good wine, hobbies, awards, good revenues, celebrations, wins, fun, exciting relationships and events, exotic trips, products, and toys—they are awesome, fun, and life enhancing. They should be enjoyed. But they will never fulfill your "searching for a connection" drive. Ultimately the new car smell goes away, the trophy tarnishes, and the new cool relationship becomes less cool. Then your internal chip returns a message that reads "still searching."

THE THREE-CORNER ROUNDABOUT

I love driving in Europe, where I get to experience the roundabout. The trick is to get off at the right exit, lest I continue to go around in a circle. I have to admit, it happens more than I would like. But it's amusing to me, and pretty harmless if it's only a few trips around.

Less amusing, though, is the trip around the Three-Corner Roundabout. You might have been there. You start in Corner One, feeling a bit alone and by yourself. You reach out, hoping for some support or a sense of partnering or community. But you have unwittingly drifted into Corner Number Two, into some kind of connection that ends up making you feel not good enough. Now you feel bad, less of something than you should be, guilty, or some other version of inferior.

Well, enough of that, right? So you do something to make yourself feel better. Let's take a trip into Corner Three, whatever your medicine of choice. You imbibe for a while, feeling some relief, and then, before too long, you make a U-turn and go back to Corner Two. Now you feel ashamed and defeated, struggling to admit that you gave in again.

And so you're back in Corner One again, feeling that you have nowhere, really, left to turn. What now?

Well, you could go back to Three . . . take another dose. And sometimes you do. And so it goes, round and round and round. You pass through the same places over and over, but you're not able to escape or find a way out. Is there anywhere else to go? And if there is, how do you get there?

Let's see. . . .

CHAPTER FOUR

GO TO CORNER FOUR

*N*eed. On the one hand, it is literally the essence of what makes life work. At the same time, it is a state that we don't relish embracing. That is the ultimate paradox in every human's life.

Think about it: at the most vital and basic level, how do you get the essential supplies that make life work, such as oxygen, water, and food? *By embracing your need for them.* Oxygen, water, and food do not kidnap you, tie you up, and force themselves upon you, invading your body against your will. They do not enter you without your permission. You give them permission to enter your system because you need them. And as you align yourself with those needs and embrace them, you breathe, drink, and eat, taking in what the outside world has to offer you. As you do, you grow and thrive. You take in what your system needs from the outside, and your system metabolizes those provisions and builds all of the vital structures of the human system.

The same is true with relationships. They are as essential as oxygen, water, and food, yet we often avoid taking them in, let alone asking for the critical fuel that relationships provide. Too often we get stuck in the Three Corners Roundabout, not being able to reach the very things that will help us thrive. We avoid embracing our needs for support and help from one another.

Psychologists call this the "need-fear" dilemma. We fear the vulnerability that it takes to embrace our needs, so they go unmet. The more we need things from people, the scarier it gets to ask for what we need. We try to manage this need in other ways, hanging out in the first three corners, which bring no good outcomes and just reinforce limits. Try as we may to hold our breath longer, eventually we will be gasping for relational air. The need does not go away. It only grows, and as it does, so does the fear of being even more vulnerable.

Fortunately, you don't have to accept the futility of a three-corner reality. There is a Corner Four, the place where real connections are made. But how can you know if it's a real connection?

THE REAL THING

In the simplest terms, a real connection is one in which you can be your whole self, the real, authentic you, a relationship to which you can bring your heart, mind, soul, and passion. Both parties to the relationship are wholly present, known, understood, and mutually invested. What each truly thinks, feels, believes, fears, and needs can be shared safely.

On the best teams, in business or in war, this is what happens. And in the best lives. No matter where you are or what obstacles you might be facing, you need your connections in order to win. They help you figure out where you are, where you need to go, where the real enemies are; they give you the reinforcements you need to win. That's what it means when someone "has your back." Like a Navy SEAL who parachutes into hostile territory, the connection that comes in Corner Four stems from three questions:

- Where am I?

- Where is the enemy?

- Where is my buddy?

No matter what the answers are to questions 1 and 2, the way out of difficulty is going to come from having the answer to question 3. If you are lost, you can connect with your buddy and find your way. If the enemy is about to get you and you're surrounded with no way out, you can call for reinforcement and your buddy will take the enemy out. If you can't find your buddy, you're in some deep stuff. You might not make it out at all. Everything ultimately hinges on each other. SEALS know that, and they train to always be there. So should we.

THE MASK OF INAUTHENTICITY

The concept of the true self versus the false self is an old construct in the field of psychology, meaning exactly what it says. The true self is who you really are, and the false self is the mask that we put on to protect ourselves.

Many CEOs and high performers have told me that their number-one challenge is the tension between the two. Because of their position, there's nowhere they can let down the mask. Former British prime minister Tony Blair once told me that one of the most difficult aspects of leadership was "the face." When I asked him what that meant, he said Bill Clinton had told him that each and every day, no matter what you are going through and how bad it is, the leader has to put on "the face"—the face of hope, strength, optimism. People are looking to the leader, he said, for all of those things, and you have to deliver confidence, no matter where you may be on the inside. The public face of leadership goes with the territory. And he's right. People need to see hope and strong determination in the faces of their leaders.

Fine . . . as long as you know it's something you're putting on for a moment because your people need it. It also has to be real. You have to truly believe in what you are saying and must in no way be lying. But that doesn't mean that you don't have *other* feelings as well—feelings like fear, discouragement, or frustration that are tucked away behind the face in that moment. The question for the leader is this: Where can you go *without* the mask? Or as a Navy SEAL would put it, where is my buddy when I need to let him know I need him?

All great leaders need to be able to address their constituents—whether voters, employees, or investors—with confidence and the courage of their convictions, but those same leaders need a safe place to nurse their wounds, to be restored, and to let down their guard and be real.

Too many leaders think that these two faces of leadership are incompatible, but as we have seen, the search for connection never ends. Everyone needs a buddy; we all need to be able to express our needs and know that they will be heard and met, that we will be relieved.

One professional organization that's put this idea into great practice is the Young President's Organization (YPO). Members are put into peer-to-peer learning groups called forums. These forums often meet once a month, for a whole day. As one CEO told me, "It has saved my life and my business more than once. It's the only place where I can be *real* [there's that word again] and let people know where I really am. And that group is there for me. They step in and help me when I need it. I value it more than any other activity I am involved in." He went on to enumerate times over the years when his group has helped him solve business problems, relationship problems, personal issues, and has been the band of buddies that got him through the hardest times of his professional and personal life.

As he put it, "No one there is invested in my results other than they care about me and want me to succeed. So, they have no agenda other than to be there for me, to help me, and I am free to bring my needs to them."

This is just one example of the power of Corner Four connections. Let's take a look at the opposite situation, in which a lack of any buddies at all came with a high price.

LOSING HEART

Liam was a renowned heart surgeon, head of a famous medical system. He had received every accolade from the medical world as a leading innovator and from the business community for his ability to make health care systems profitable.

He called me at the literal height of his career. "I need to talk to you," he said. "I have a problem."

We blocked out a day for him to fly to Los Angeles, and he told me a painful story.

"What brings you here?" I asked.

"I have made some big mistakes," he said. "Mistakes that can ruin everything, and I need to fix it."

He went on to tell me a story of Corner Three behavior involving several extramarital affairs over a number of years—with nurses, hospital staff, and others. His wife had recently found out, as well as the board of two of the medical systems that he was leading. Needless to say, there were serious ripple effects—more like a tsunami, actually.

His wife moved out. His hospital ties and investors were threatened. His partners found themselves having to address very difficult HR issues, to say the least. His four children were hurt and disillusioned. On and on the destructive damage gathered, on both the personal and business sides of life.

Not surprisingly, he was personally devastated as well. Even before getting caught, he had been in hell, living two lives: a leader in his field and community, on the one hand, and a cheater and liar on the other. As he put it, "I'm glad it all came to light, even in such a painful way, because it was killing me." (In fact, his grown daughter and her husband had caught him in a lie, were curious, followed his car, and found him with a woman.)

Which brings us to the moment that is the point of this story.

"I came here to see you," he said, "so you could give me some input about my plan. I want to turn everything around, save my marriage, and really change. So, I have made some serious commitments and put some things in place that I think are going to help, and I want to get your thoughts on my plan."

He was hopeful; he said his wife was agreeable to working things out if he was really serious about changing his behavior. Otherwise, she was done. So far so good, I thought. I asked, "What's the plan?"

"Well, I've made a commitment to Susan to be a better husband and attend to her needs more," he began. "I can see how I kind of check out when I'm not working . . . there is so much stress with what I do. Sometimes I ignore her emotional needs, and I am going to stop doing that."

Liam described the incredible stress he felt in performing high-risk surgeries, "It is *so* easy to kill these people," he blurted out. "The amount of stress I live with is crazy, . . . but it's the nature of the work. I have to be so careful and right. All the time."

He admitted that by the time he came home from work, he just wanted a few martinis and a chance to veg out. But now he proposed to change things. "I'm committed to being a better companion. Each night we're going to take walks and have dinner together, and I am going to focus on listening to her," he explained. "Plus, I've agreed to go to marriage counseling to try to learn to be what she needs and work on our relationship. To do better."

He described other aspects of his ambitious plan, which included reading spiritual material each day, eating better, exercising more, and changing other aspects of his lifestyle. "But mostly," he added, "it's centered on being a better husband, making sure I'm giving her what she needs and what I've ignored," he emphasized. "I have a checklist of things I'm committed to doing for her and am living by it."

As I listened, thinking that all of these things were indeed wonderful elements of a life well lived—closeness with his spouse, spiritual discipline, a healthy lifestyle, marriage counseling, diligence in his commitment to her, and the rest—I was becoming more and more depressed. Not because he didn't need to make all of those changes. He did. I was getting depressed for one simple reason: *The plan was going to fail.* Guaranteed, as sure as we were sitting there.

I felt for him as he relayed his plan, and I felt for her because of the next train wreck that was certainly headed her way.

"So what do you think?" he asked.

"Want the truth?" I asked back.

"Of course," he said.

"I think you're headed for another heart attack, to use your language."

Startled, he asked, "What do you mean?"

I said, "I think you've probably had this very same conversation with hundreds of your heart patients. They have a heart attack, and then don't address the lifestyle issues that caused the heart disease, and you know it is going to happen again. You can see it coming."

"But I'm making a lot of changes," he retorted. "A *lot*!"

"I know . . . and that's what scares me," I answered. "The

changes you're making are all going to make the disease worse, not better. You're adding more and more to the problem, not fixing it."

"How?" he asked.

"Every strategy you're using involves more *output* from you. More giving. More discipline. More obedience to what is right. More effort. More service and sacrifice. *This whole thing depends on you, and it's not going to work.*"

"But . . . why? Those are the things I need to do to make it different," he said.

I regained my patience and explained that although his list addressed the problems in the marriage, they wouldn't fix the underlying problem that caused his sexual acting out in the first place. "You will do that again," I warned him, "if this is your plan. I promise you."

"But why? I really am committed to not doing that anymore," he said.

I believed him. But there is a fundamental problem with this approach: the whole plan depended on his performance and his output. I said as much to him: "In short, it depends on *your strength* to make it work. It's based on *your* ability. *Your* output. That's the problem. You have been acting out of *your* needs, *your* weaknesses, and *your* vulnerabilities. And you still have those needs, weaknesses, and vulnerabilities. They have not gone away. And this strategy has nothing to do with bringing fulfillment to those needs, strength to those weaknesses, and help to the places in your soul where you feel vulnerable."

Nothing in his plan, I observed, suggested how he would be receiving any help for *his* needs or meeting them in any way. The entire plan was about expressing strength and nothing about *building* strength. It was as if a car runs out of gas, and the remedy is for the car to give itself some "self-gas" and drive better.

Liam's problems weren't caused by his strengths, but by his weaknesses, his vulnerabilities, and his unmet needs. I suspected that if we were to look back through his personal history, we'd find a long list of gold stars, commendations, and medals for service— and that is all good. But I doubt that we'd find many instances of Liam's vulnerability and depending on others for strength, encouragement, or support.

"The only encouragement you probably get," I suggested, "is when you perform well, by way of awards and trophies." As Liam shook his head in agreement, I pointed out that real encouragement comes when you are feeling discouraged, weak, or down, and need *help from someone else*. In the absence of that, Liam had gone looking for comfort and connection in all the wrong places, in the arms of a lot of women. "That was a place where you could truly let down your guard," I pointed out, "and someone was there just for you. Not demanding anything from you, just there to gratify you—the exact opposite of your regular fourteen-hour day, when you're there for everyone else," I said.

He just kind of looked at me. Silent. Staring into the middle distance . . . no words. It was strange for a moment, how stunned he looked.

So I asked, "Do you remember ever needing and depending on others?" This is when it got really interesting.

He looked into space for a moment and then said that something had brought a lot of different strands of experience and memories together for him. "I just remembered something that might have to do with what you are talking about," he said.

"What?" I asked.

"It's going to sound weird, but it may be what you're getting at. When I was about sixteen, my father's drinking had come to a head and he had to go into rehab. It was something we always had around us, but no one ever really talked about it. We just stepped around it. And then, finally, he had to go into treatment. It was like something big and ominous had happened.

"Then, while he was there, my mother had a nervous breakdown and had to be hospitalized. They told us she was going away for a long time. I had two little sisters and two little brothers. That night, when my parents had gone, I remember walking out into the yard and looking at the sky, wondering what I was going to do from there. I remember this like it was yesterday. . . . I thought almost out loud . . . I might have even said it out loud. 'There's no one to depend on anymore. It's all going to be up to me,'" he said solemnly.

Liam realized that that was how he'd lived ever since: taking care of his siblings and everyone else, busting his butt through college, and training for eight years to be a cardiac surgeon without complaint. It was all output.

I suggested that what he was describing sounded a lot like what happens when the human heart stops working, an example he would certainly understand.

"OK," I said. "Try this analogy. Doesn't a human heart have four pipes? Two coming in and two coming out?"

"Yes . . . kind of, but go ahead," he said.

"So it's as if you have two clogged veins. You're always pumping out, giving out, but nothing ever comes in," I said, instructing one of the leading heart surgeons of our day on how his metaphorical heart works. "Your entire life is performance, giving out and never taking in, in terms of what you need to thrive. At some point, *something* has to give. You begin to look for some way to meet those needs and get something coming in. Get comfort—care. You found a pretty good way. One that a lot of high-output performers have depended on for eons: sex. And it works, for a while. The problem is that it never is enough to meet those unmet emotional needs, just sexual needs. You always need more, like a drug. And the other problem is that now it has real consequences for your life—your marriage, your career, everything that matters to you."

Liam had gotten into trouble by ignoring his need for help from the outside, from others, and now, to fix it, he had constructed a program for his marriage and health that is once again built on, and solely dependent on, his own solitary strengths. "You have to come up with an answer that is actually the problem itself: it all depends on you. You're back to that night in high school."

"So . . . what would your plan look like?" he asked.

I proposed that he look for help outside himself—just as when people can't fix their own hearts, they call in an expert. They don't do it themselves.

"Look at it this way. How did you become a great surgeon? By yourself? No. You made yourself vulnerable and you went to others to help you. They imparted their knowledge, their expertise. They modeled it for you. They taught you. They corrected you when you made mistakes. When you felt like you couldn't do one more week of residency with multiple surgeries around the clock, they came alongside you and encouraged you. When you lost your first patient, they walked you through it. When you needed to learn the newest technique or piece of equipment or treatment protocol, someone came along and helped you. The truth is that you are who you are, highly successful in that arena, because the power of other people has helped you get there. But in those areas, it was a lot easier for you to show vulnerability. No one expects a first-year resident to know how to do a heart transplant. It was easier for you to ask for help. And I'm positive that your patients are glad you're not a 'self-made surgeon.' You learned from the best. Now you just have to figure out how to do that same thing in the rest of your life, and not be a 'self-made human.'"

A DIFFERENT PLAN

One year later, the doctor and I spoke again. When he had first come to visit me, I had put together a very different kind of plan than his, one that focused on building Corner Four connections, and he had followed it with gusto. As a result, Liam was able to get his career and his marriage back to health. He had joined an SAA (Sex Addicts Anonymous) group, as well as a high performer's support group; he had undertaken individual coaching and counseling and was attending weekly marriage counseling sessions with his wife. With his SAA group, he also had a sponsor he could call anytime, with whom he was meeting for lunch once a week, as well.

It was a lot, especially for a surgeon with his level of responsibility. But here is what he told me: "I have to tell you, my entire life is different. One year ago, you told me that my plan was not going to work. I had no idea at the time what you were talking about, but I trusted you because you have seen a lot of people like me over the years. It was the moment that led to the big moment of clarity: *I was going to have to find recovery in a different mode of thinking that required me to face my weaknesses and vulnerabilities, and reach outside for help."*

Liam recounted how, with the help of experts, he'd realized that he had been relying on self-medicating patterns of behaviors that had gotten in the way of his work, his marriage, and his family life. In the end, he'd had to "surrender" to the fact that he did have needs and that he needed other people to help him.

As Liam opened up to others, sharing his fears and insecurities, he'd had another big realization: a lot of top achievers struggle with the same issues. "I learned also from them as I listened to them . . . as they shared their issues, I learned about my own, and what I needed to do. Hearing their stories was really helpful for me."

Another important aspect of his recovery was accountability. To know that others will be checking in with you to see how you're doing brings an important resource to the plan. When your struggles are no longer a secret, a problem that only you are addressing, you can find solutions and support through others' words of encouragement. Liam summed it up like this: "The big problem with people like me is that we think we're gladiators. We can fight our way through anything and just never will give up. But when it comes to our needs, or vulnerabilities or weaknesses, that's where the gladiator mentality falls short. We can't do it alone." Bingo.

ACCESSING YOUR NEEDS

Corner Four is a place where people have true connection, where they can be authentic—not copied, not false or imitation, as Webster's defines *authentic*. When you can find a place to be authentic, you gain access to the resources that have been wanting. Finally, *the fuel and fulfillment can get to the need*.

A Navy SEAL needs strength he doesn't have . . . until he spots a buddy on the shore who gives him an encouraging fist pump.

A leading surgeon needs repair, recovery, and renewal . . . then finds wisdom and support from others on the path.

Michael Phelps needed to surpass his limits to win the most Olympic medals in history . . . then found a coach in Bob Bowman.

Whether in sports, business, or the military, it is the power of the other that always makes the difference. When discussing leadership in chapter 15 of his book *The Virgin Way*, Richard Branson quotes Zig Ziglar, who said this before neuroscience could explain how it works: "A lot of people have gone further than they thought they could because someone else thought they could." Early in his business career, Branson was taken under the wing of a mentor friend of his parents, David Beevers. He spent one evening a week with Beevers gaining business guidance. Beevers even helped Branson learn the fundamentals of financial accounting. What if the young entrepreneur had not been able to reveal his need for help? To be authentic about what he didn't know? What if out of fear of being vulnerable he had gone into Corner One and isolated himself? Or Corner Two and tried to prove himself? Or Corner Three and medicated himself with sex or a substance? There would be no Virgin. Instead, he authentically reached into Corner Four for strength.

Further along on his path of building Virgin Airlines, Branson turned to an established veteran in the airline world, Freddie Laker. From teaching him how to compete with giants such as British Airways when you have no money (try that one), to showing him how to launch Virgin Atlantic "with zero experience whatsoever in the airline industry," Laker is credited by Branson as the mentor who helped him make it all work: "I wouldn't have gotten anywhere in the airline industry without Freddie's down-to-earth wisdom."

Think about it.

- Henry Ford had Thomas Edison.

- Mark Zuckerberg was mentored by Steve Jobs.

- Bill Gates had Warren Buffet and Ed Roberts.

- Jack Nicklaus had Jack Grout.

- Michael Jordan had Phil Jackson.

- Bill Hewlett and David Packard had Frederick Terman.

- Sheryl Sandberg had Larry Summers.

There is no such thing as a self-made man or woman. Every great leader has opened up to someone who could meet a need, whatever that might have been. The range of human needs is broad, but *the way to meet those needs is very narrow*: it involves humbly and honestly embracing the need and reaching out to the "power of the other." There is no other way.

In the more than twenty-five years I've been working with high-powered CEOs and other top performers, one characteristic stands out: the leaders who accomplish the most, thrive the most, overcome the most are *not afraid to say they need help*. Most of them have come to me of their own volition—the so-called self-referred, as opposed to those leaders who've been required to get coaching by their bosses or boards. They show up with an agenda, a list of things they want help with. Some of them are running Fortune 25 companies, overseeing billions and billions, and they say, "I need some help with . . ." I'm often awed by their humility. What a privilege to hear a truly great leader get vulnerable, and say, "I need some help with this." I often feel a welling up inside at the beauty and power of their authenticity. It is simple honesty about what one needs, even if that person is "great" at so many things.

Naturally, I've also met with the other kind of leader: the ones who don't really want to be there getting help, who can't or won't embrace what they need. They have all the answers. As they often put it, they "don't really need help, but my board wants me to talk to you." In the past, I have done my best to turn their resistance into some kind of growth and insight . . . something, *anything*. And that has value; it is noble work. But lately I feel like Danny Glover in the movie *Lethal Weapon*. When he and Mel Gibson are getting shot at, he exclaims, "I'm too old for this shit!" Trying to think of ways to get someone to see their need for help is not something I want to do anymore. I want to spend my time with those who want it. Why? Because they are the only ones who will grow, who will get better. And here is the real learning: they are always the best anyway! The best ones, the greatest performers, are the humble ones who know what they need and express it freely.

This is one of the biggest problems with board of directors and sometimes with executive teams. Sometimes a leader will put together a board or team of yes-men. They are totally behind the leader, which is good, but the equation is off. *The leader can't humble himself to receive help, and the board is afraid to tell him he needs it.* The emperor has no clothes, and no one is telling him!

But then there are the real superstars, the ones with enormous talent and brains who realize that they don't have all it takes to get big things done but that everything they need to get them done does exist—in others. So they *ask*. They *need*. They embrace their need, and they connect from an authentic, vulnerable place. They grow. They learn. They thrive. I love getting to work with that kind of person.

Be one of those, no matter where you are. Humble yourself. Head to Corner Four and seek someone who can meet the need that you have. Whether for emotional support, courage, wisdom, expertise, or pure community, go to Corner Four . . . and stay there.

CHAPTER FIVE

THE FUEL FOR HIGH PERFORMANCE

Have you ever had one of those surprises that rocks your world? When you find out that everything you thought was wrong, and that reality is the opposite of what you understood it to be? If you have been in business very long, you probably have. They are not fun. A friend of mine, for example, bought a chain of hamburger outlets in another part of the country, and then decided to actually go visit some of them. He found that many of them were falling down and dilapidated, not nearly what he had thought he had purchased.

I had one of those experiences too, and it was one of the worst days of my business life. I owned a company that I had hired someone to run and for which I had great hopes. I had spun off some other parts of it, gotten great assets out of it, and thought I was off to the races. The person I had put in charge had come to my attention through a referral; his background and experience were exactly what I thought the company needed to go to the next level. It was an exciting time . . . until it wasn't.

It was early December when he showed up at my office, asking me to immediately put a big infusion of cash into the company in order to make payroll and pay other expenses. I could not believe my ears. For several months, he had been giving me reports with projections indicating that by the end of the year we would have made a lot of money, and there would be pretty substantial cash disbursements. I was ready to get a big check, and now he was telling me that if we were going to stay in business, I was going to have to write one.

My first thought, even though in that particular business I didn't see how it was possible, was that we had a lot of receivables out there and he was just in a cash-flow crunch. Obviously he just needed some short-term financing until the money came in. I just needed to find out more of the facts so we could solve this, and then I would get my profits.

But—and these kinds of stories always have a *but*—as I spent the rest of the day uncovering the rest of the picture, I realized I'd been standing on quicksand. Not only were there very few receivables headed our way; there was little revenue, either. Virtually *all* of the business he said we had booked for the next year were not booked at all. It was just "planned." Little in writing, no deposits, no confirmations. It was all business that he was working on, but in truth did not exist. And then the really bad news hit me: *there were no profits from the current year, either.* He had been running up losses, and we were in significant debt to many suppliers and vendors. It was the worst scenario possible: underwater financially, nothing in the pipeline, and a serious burn rate going forward. I was in shock.

But not only was I really distressed about the business; I was also devastated personally. I felt like a total idiot. I couldn't believe I had made such a big blunder. I had hired someone without really doing all of the due diligence I should have done; I just had some friends' word about him and had taken his résumé at face value. I should have taken more time and talked to more people. The more I thought about it, though, the more I recognized that the context in which he had achieved earlier success was very different from the one I'd put him in, so some of the factors that had made him successful before were not in this picture. I should have seen that.

Worse, I had ignored some instincts I'd had about him as well. I just overlooked them, thinking that he would be able to do what I needed him to do, as his résumé said, even if my gut was telling me not to be so sure. Probably worst of all, I had not gotten deep enough into the operations for a while and had been too much of an absentee owner.

Wow, did I feel bad. I looked at the mess I had created and felt horrible and, even worse, disheartened about the future. It was going to take a long time to dig my way out, if the business could even be saved. All I could think was *What an idiot I've been! How could I have let this happen?*

Then it got even worse. I was at home that evening, standing on my patio, when the phone rang. I didn't feel like answering it, but in the midst of the crisis, I thought I'd better see who it was.

This was before caller ID, so you actually had to pick up a phone to see who was there. When I picked it up, I instantly regretted it, as I recognized the voice.

"What's happening?" my friend asked.

It was my main business mentor at that time, one of the most influential people in my life. When I had gotten out of graduate school, he had taken me under his wing and taught me more about business than I could have gotten in three MBAs. He was extremely successful in several industries, from finance to entertainment to real estate to high tech. In my eyes, he had done it all and had always done it well.

My heart sank. Here I was in the middle of the biggest failure I had ever had, and Superman happens to call me right in that moment. Why couldn't it be some loser who was calling me, not someone who always seemed to do it right? And why did it have to be the one person who had poured so much time and energy into me, teaching me how to do it right as well? I was ashamed of where I was and ashamed that I was going to have to admit it all to him.

"Well . . . a lot." I answered. "And it's not good. In fact, it's pretty bad."

"What's going on?" he asked.

"I have really screwed up," I confessed. I proceeded to tell him the entire story. I had blown it. Really blown it.

He was silent on the other end of the line. I was waiting for him to just rip into me and scold me for what I had done. And then he said it: "Well, we've all been there."

Wait . . . what did he say? I thought, *Did he say "we"? As in, him too?*

"Who? Been where?" I asked.

"We've all made that mistake," he said. "We've all hired the wrong person or done a deal with the wrong partner, when we should have seen it coming. And paid dearly for it."

"*You've* done that??" I asked. I could not believe what I was hearing.

"Absolutely," he said. "Anyone who has built anything or done anything significant has made that mistake. We've all had to learn that one."

As we continued talking, as he understood and cared, something happened in me. Something huge. In the course of a few moments. Something I could not even explain. Something that it would be years later before neuroscience could explain for me.

From the outside, the situation was still as bleak as before he called. But I *felt* different. Something cleared in my head. I could feel the thinking machine turning on again. I felt some *energy* that I had not felt before in the black cloud that had been hanging over me. I don't know how to describe it, other than to say I was just *different*. It was similar to that moment when you have been really, really sick, and the fever breaks or the medicine kicks in, and all of a sudden, you feel almost restored to health. It was like some light breaking through in a dark storm. What had happened?

Now we know from science that I was getting "well" because of his empathy, his ability to connect with me and show me that he understood, that he identified with me, and that he was *for* me. My brain chemistry was changing. The effects of the stress hormones that had been interfering with my thinking were lessening. My higher-order thinking machine was getting refueled with the kinds of chemicals (neurotransmitters, the fuel of the brain) that it needs to run.

Emotionally, I felt less discouraged for several reasons, not the least of which was the combination of not feeling like the only idiot on the planet who would ever do such a lame thing, but also because I'd caught a glimpse of hope. The conversation with my buddy had shown me that I could come back from this mess, as he had . . . that there could be better days coming. Physically, I felt different too. I could feel the energy come back, preparing me to push forward into finding an answer.

Nothing about the situation had changed. Except one thing: I had tapped into the power of the other. After our talk, I now had energy and the courage to get to work. My tank was full.

We can feel how our physical and mental energy shifts when we form a connection with someone, but it is still hard for us to truly accept how real this transfer of energy and ability actually is. What exactly is this thing that causes us to gear up or wind down? As Dr. Siegel puts it, "What is the 'thing' that is actually being regulated, the something that is shared by the body and by our relational communication? The answer is *energy*."

Dr. Siegel has spent years trying to understand these processes. Among other things, the big finding is this:

Relationship, the connection between people, not only enhances our mental functioning, but actually works to *impart* it, to *provide* it. Capacity is built through energy and intelligence. I love the definition of energy that Siegel uses, borrowing a phrase from physicists. It is "the capacity to do something."

Speaking of which, I really needed to do something to save my business. But first I needed to regain some of the capacity I'd lost. Just as the Navy SEAL regained the capacity to finish the swim when Mark connected with him, I got a similar infusion of energy from my friend's phone call. The abilities of my body, my psyche, my emotional self, and a lot of other parts of me changed as a result. With this new injection of energy, I was able to get past feeling dejected and defeated and was able to start to address the situation.

REFUELING

The energy derived from relationships isn't something that's easy to fully understand, even though it has become clear, through practical experience and neuroscience, that it has very real effects.

I once went to the finals of *The Voice*, the singing-competition TV show. We were all sitting there in the auditorium waiting for the competition to begin when a guy comes out who was something between a cheerleader, a comedian, and a lightning bolt. He got us all energized, clapping, hooting and hollering. The place was transformed. At the same time, the producer was going around connecting and inspiring everyone on the set.

Then, with a high energy crowd, the music began, Carson Daly came out, and the show got under way. By the time the performers entered the scene, the energy was palpable. (If we'd had the right equipment on-site, we probably could have scanned the audience's brains to see the effects.) I have no doubt it made a difference in how the performers did. The person, or the band, who warms up the crowd serves an important function. Their routines are *not* just filler, but a source of fuel that drives the entire experience, for members of the audience and the performers alike.

Noel Tichy is a leadership expert and was a consultant to GE in the Jack Welch days. In his book *The Leadership Engine* (Harper-Collins, 2009), he wrote, "All organizations inherently have energy because they are made up of people, and people have energy. But in winning organizations, people seem to have more energy, and they certainly use it more productively. While the losers waste their energy on negative activities such as internal politics and resisting changes demanded by the marketplace, the winners use theirs positively to overcome problems and meet new challenges. They do this because their top leaders understand that positive energy produces positive results. They use energy, like ideas and values, as a competitive tool."

Tichy makes an important point. Fuel is not always about high energy *action*, yelling at people, or getting them riled up. When I faced my own business crisis, for example, my mentor didn't yell at all, nor did he try to sugarcoat the situation. He didn't say what my World War II–veteran father used to tell me: "Well, that's no hill for a climber." Instead, he connected with me where I was at that moment, and the result was an infusion of energy.

The true fuel of performance comes first from the experience of connectedness that is available only in Corner Four, where you experience the other as being *with* you, and *for* you. This is what neuroscience and researchers like Dr. Siegel have shown over and over. In some situations, though, refueling requires more than just a quiet, understanding listener. Sometimes it must be action oriented, as well. Think of it this way: sometimes you have to push a car with a dead battery to pop the clutch so it can start. These are the times when we need a wake-up call from the people who truly care about us in our Corner Four.

So many times we confuse this issue. We think that the real and genuinely supportive relationships of Corner Four deal only in happy thoughts and are always "positive." They *are* positive in their intent and their desired result, but sometimes there is a *lot* of negative stuff that is talked about. If we're not getting it or not performing in some way, our Corner Four people sometimes have to wake us up and be pretty tough. They have to say some hard things, which sometimes hurt to hear, but just like the cut of a surgeon's knife that saves a life, a friend's tough but kind message can save our lives as well. We need these kick starts and truth moments in order to get to our next level.

Recently I was in an executive team meeting where we had discussed the Four Corners. After understanding this point, the chief marketing officer said, "OK, so we are all in Corner Four here, right? So, there is something I have to say about the way we have been looking at this project." He then went on to say some pretty hard things for some to hear, but it went well. It had helped that they had just talked about this very issue—that in Corner Four we care about each other *and* we say the truth. We take it constructively, not personally. Very powerful stuff, when everyone understands the truth telling of a caring Corner Four.

INFORMATION AND LEARNING BRING ENERGY

Another way to bring new energy into your system is by gathering new information. That often comes in the form of a new connection, a new relationship with someone who brings in a different set of skills, knowledge, and expertise. When a floundering team gets a new member, that person brings in new knowledge, intelligence and insights that release new energy into the group. The whole team is lifted up.

Especially when it comes to self-improvement—like weight loss or overcoming an addiction—we need the energy of a community to stay with the program in a way that fuels us. Research has shown that if you are in a community that is getting healthy or overcoming something difficult, your chances of success go way, way up. This explains why groups like Weight Watchers and other support systems are so successful. They surround you with people who all are heading in a healthy direction, and that positive energy is contagious. The same is true for other goal-oriented paths. The more we are surrounded by people who are motivated to get there, the more we catch that energy and are moved toward success ourselves.

When you add information and learning, the energy only goes up. The learning curve and peer pressure to keep up is very healthy. The same dynamic happens in growth settings as well. In Weight Watchers, for example, if people are going to the groups, they are not only getting support, but also gaining new knowledge about life change that fuels them.

If you are a business leader, please make sure to take your teams and people to off-site learning experiences, leadership conferences, continuing education, and the like. Place them in cross-functional assignments, and lend them out to other bosses, departments, and companies. Keep the learning high, and you will keep the energy high as well. Jack Welch is known for injecting this learning energy into GE. I interviewed him once at Leadercast and asked him about this. He said that he spent more than half his time at GE *teaching leadership*! Think of that: one of the biggest companies in the world, and the CEO is using his time to *teach his leaders*. But the energy advantage that a learning organization has over a stagnant one is huge.

There are simple ways to do this. Just get a good leadership book every month, have the team read it, and take a little time once a week to discuss what you all are learning. Watch the energy go up.

THE RIGHT KIND OF ENERGY

The takeaway is a practical approach to emotional energy. In your personal life, what kind of energy are you surrounding yourself with? Positive or negative? Goal-oriented or stagnant? Healthy or unhealthy? Where are your Corner Four fueling stations? Whom do you catch the energy or growth from? In your professional life, ask yourself the same questions. Who brings fuel to you? Who brings the energy of new intelligence, support, and other provisions? We all need that kind of fueling, and it's important to know where we're going to get it.

I was recently planning an off-site with a CEO to work through some very difficult decisions, and I encouraged him to make sure that a certain person would not be included in the gathering. Surprised at my suggestion, the CEO asked, "Why not? He knows a lot about this market."

"I know," I said. "But this group has got to begin to get creative, get motivated to take the next steps, and that requires creative energy, positive energy. Whatever he brings in knowledge will be discounted by the amount of negative energy he unleashes on the group."

"Oh my gosh! That's exactly right," he agreed.

Whether as a leader, a parent, or a spouse, think about whether the dynamic you're creating will help release positive or negative energy. I'm talking not just about what kind of energy you personally bring to these encounters, but also what kind of energy others bring. For instance, I always am monitoring and thinking about my teenage girls' peer groups and friends. I want them hanging around with life-giving, positive, loving, and encouraging kids. As a parent, these are the sorts of relationships you want your kids to invest in. Energy is contagious, so why not ensure, to the extent that you can, that the energy you allow in your kids' lives propels them forward and lifts them up?

Look at your own life and work right now. Are you surrounding yourself with people who fuel you? As the steward of your life, make sure that you have these kinds of Corner Four "fueling stations" in your life, at regular intervals. For example, I have a small group that I meet with regularly, and I know that no matter how I'm doing at the time, after I'm with them, I'm going to feel and function better. I'm certain of that. Do that audit for yourself.

Similarly, start paying attention to those who drain your energy. I'm not suggesting some sort of self-centered, faux–New Age attitude where suddenly you say to someone, "I'm sorry, but I'm sensing negative energy here, and I do not allow that into my life," then walk away and lose the person's number. Spare us all from people who never want to be inconvenienced by "negative energy" (although there are relationships for which a necessary ending is

essential!). We can't and shouldn't always walk away from tough situations, obviously. Being a fruitful person, the kind of person who
actually changes the world around you, means that you sometimes
intentionally enter negative situations and work hard to transform
them. You are not afraid of problems or "problem people," so you
can't, nor should you try to, avoid all negativity. Embrace it and, as
much as you are able to influence change, inject a positive influence.
Be a change agent, if possible.

However, it is still very important to know who the drains are
in your life, why you're spending time with them, and what their
impact is. It's also important to know what your strategy is going
to be to make sure that you are not *infected* in these encounters.
Remember, sometimes doctors wear masks to avoid getting and
giving infections. With some highly virulent conditions, they wear
hazmat suits! So if you're encountering some really negative energy,
even if by necessity or on purpose, just make sure that you've taken
precautions to avoid getting infected. We hear a lot about "managing your energy" these days. That's important, but it's not just
about managing your workload and taking breaks; it's just as important to manage the *energy sources* around you. This is intensely
interpersonal. People give energy, and they take it away. Know the
difference and plan accordingly.

Another source of energy and new information for leaders
is what I call the listening tour. These are structured, intentional
interactions or touchpoints with employees meant to identify the
sources of negative energy that may be affecting an individual's,
a team's, or the company's performance. I encourage the leader to
listen and work through topics that have become a drain to employees, especially in areas where the company itself and its leadership

have enacted policies or strategies that have caused difficulty and distress. Don't shy away from addressing the negative energy. That alone—listening—brings positive energy to the group and can begin to transform it.

I've seen it work in a variety of situations. In one case, there was a real gap between the home office and the field. The listening tour, conducted by the COO, helped clear up miscommunication and rebuild trust. It raised the energy of the branch-office teams, who felt emboldened to come up with solutions of their own to confront their challenges. They literally thought at higher levels. Why? Because their "thinker" changed through new energy infusion.

At first, this can seem like a big commitment, but when you see the results, you realize what an important and relatively easy bet it is. Like any good investment, the rewards increase over time. One leader I work with structures a dozen or more of these listening-tour meetings through various regions during a year. I go with him, and that is what we do. We listen. The results are huge.

DIFFERENT STROKES

Just as there are positive and negative sources of energy, there are also different "brands" or "flavors" of energy we need to fuel professional and personal growth. For one's own sake and as an other to someone else, it's important to know what brand of energy a person needs to fuel growth.

In other books I've written, I've talked about a period in my life when the power of the other saved me and helped me find my life's work. The short version is that I had been recruited to play college golf and was looking forward to pursuing that dream when I went to school. In my first week at college, however, I developed a hand injury that hampered my play for the next two years and eventually resulted in my having to quit the game I had loved since childhood. At the same time, I went through a painful breakup with my girlfriend and discovered the onset of a prediabetic condition that was leading to migraines. I became extremely depressed and discouraged. For months, I stumbled around, half dazed, trying to pick myself up and get on with life. But my efforts led nowhere except into deeper depression, and finally I was forced to take a semester off to figure out what I was going to do.

I discovered that getting well, getting on with life, and thriving again was not going to be something I could do on my own. First, a fraternity brother of mine reached out to help me, and also introduced me to his older sister and her husband, who was a seminary student. When I say, "They took me in," I mean it literally. They asked me to move in with them, and they brought me back to life out of a dark time, until I could return to school.

That "fueling" was multidimensional. It was the emotional, intellectual, physical, purposeful, and spiritual energy I needed to get going again. With the help of this couple, a good therapist, and a small group of friends, I got back on a much healthier physical path, through eating differently, getting enough rest, and establishing a healthy activity level that I had fallen out of in my depression. Intellectually, they introduced me to books about growth and a whole new world of ideas that I had never seen before in philosophy and theology. I was reading book after book and going to workshops and classes that were exposing me to more growth, both personally and intellectually, than I had ever experienced in all of my years of conventional schooling. This intense intellectual growth was as energizing as all of the sports I had ever played.

They worked hard on me emotionally, as well. I had gone through a lot, and they encouraged me to talk it all through, learn from it, and establish new patterns that were much healthier. They focused on emotional intelligence well before that term was popularized. It was painful at times, as all Corner Four relationships must be to do their work, but I probably grew up more in that time than ever before. The *fueling* they gave me was enormous, providing a foundation for all that I do now. The meaning I'd found was even greater than the satisfaction I'd gotten in competitive golfing. They infused me back to life.

I share this story again to remind you that fuel, and especially the fuel that we get from Corner Four relationships, comes from many *different* dimensions of life. Corner Four relationships affect us physically, emotionally, intellectually, and spiritually as they help us find our purpose in life. In most cases, no one relationship can supply our needs in all of these dimensions, though sometimes one is paramount. That's why it's important to establish multiple connections that feed us different kinds of energy. It does "take a village" to grow a person, and to sustain one.

Some of the most fascinating and rewarding experiences I have as a leadership coach are working with CEOs, executive teams, and other leaders when they take time away from work to focus on mission, purpose, and values. Values are like rocket fuel when worked on in an ongoing process. Too many businesses write up some values and slap them on a wall, but never revisit them. I love getting into a process with a company wherein we develop an internal strategic plan to come up with the values that actually fuel the performance of the mission and engage everyone deeply in these discussions as the company does its work. When a team develops a cadence of not only coming up with values but working on *making them real* over time, the energy that comes into that business is remarkable. In these cases, the values aren't posters on a wall. They are living behavioral and interpersonal practices that bring the power of the other to the equation, and that changes individuals, teams, departments, and organizations.

EARLY WARNING SIGNS

If you were in an airplane, the gauges would tell you when you were in trouble. If you're running low on fuel, you get a warning light. Heading in the wrong direction, you get another kind of warning. Oil pressure drops, and an alarm sounds. Knowing where you are and the state of your plane is key to staying in the air.

Same thing with your cell phone, remember? It shows you the bars. It shows you when you have lost connection and it is searching. It has a low-battery warning, as well as a "limited connection" at times. It tells you, "Install update."

These gauges and dashboards are there to let you know the current state of things that need your attention before you get into trouble. It's the same with the question, "Where are you?" If you don't know where you are—emotionally and in relation to others—you're going to have trouble keeping the plane in the air. Fortunately, there are signs you can look out for.

The disconnection of Corner One can offer temporary relief, especially when you are under stress and things are not going well. It's an easy retreat, but it's also deceptive. Don't get me wrong: Solitude can be incredibly fueling in and of itself, especially for introverts. The ability to be alone, comfortably and contentedly, is an important step toward emotional maturity and health. But solitude is not Corner One isolation. Isolation won't give you a chance to refuel but merely offers a temporary escape. If you find yourself heading into Corner One as a way to avoid conflict and intimacy while wrongly calling it alone time, you'll end up with loss of energy and drive. So watch out. A good test? If you go for solitude, do you still have real, connecting, honest, and vulnerable Corner Four time with others that addresses what you thought about while alone? If you are sharing it at some point, your solitude is probably in service of refueling and sorting things out in your quiet time alone. But if you are not, you might be in Corner One isolation and just calling it solitude or introversion.

You can also spot the signs of trouble in Corner Two. When alarm bells in your head start ringing, "You're not good enough," when fear—of disapproval, of displeasing someone, or of falling short of some metric of goodness—starts driving your actions, you know you're running out of fuel.

The pull to seek something that makes you feel "good"—that's Corner Three on the map—is another warning sign. If you find yourself itching for comfort in illicit relationships, addictive substances, or other compulsive behavior, you know you're risking stalemate at best, and eventually a big crash. Don't trust anything that feels good if it isn't something you'd want your spouse, partner, family, or your colleagues to know about. Or if it doesn't fulfill you in and of itself, meaning that if you just need more of it again soon afterward in order to be gratified, it is probably more addicting than it is nourishing. And if it doesn't require you to be your authentic self, then it's probably fake anyway.

Whenever these alarms start going off, seek out Corner Four. Be honest about where you are and what you need when you get there. That's where all the good stuff is.

CHAPTER SIX

FREEDOM AND CONTROL

Jack Nicklaus is the greatest golfer the world has ever known. His record of major wins is unsurpassed, even years after his last victory. Winning eighteen major tournaments is a record that is likely to stand for a long time. For those of you who are not golfers, that is the equivalent of more Super Bowls, World Series, heavyweight championships, tennis Grand Slams, or any other sports crown won by a single person or team. If you're not a sports person, just call it the Oscars and think Katharine Hepburn.

In building that record of achievement, in my view, one trait, one ability, mattered more than any other: his will to win, to hit the shot that had to be hit, to make the putt that had to be made. As more than one commentator has noted, when Nicklaus made a putt to win a tournament, he just *willed* it into the hole. He had what seemed to be unparalleled self-control that translated into making things happen: wins. He embodies the essence of performance—the ability to make it happen.

Of all of his feats, one stands out to me. It was in the 1972 U.S. Open at Pebble Beach. On the seventeenth hole, he faced what he described as a howling wind, a 218-yard shot, and a three-stroke lead, which on a hole like that could quickly disappear. What happened? He hit the shot. The ball *hit the flagstick* and fell a few inches from the hole. Birdie! And a locked-up U.S. Open victory. (Google it. You will watch it several times.)

In a career spanning so many years and so many victories, why does that one shot stand out to me above all others?

SELF-CONTROL

Here's the rest of the story.

Nicklaus has described what happened in that historic moment. Right at the beginning of his backswing, the wind howls and forces his swing somewhat off-line. He can feel that it's not right. So what does he do? *He adjusts his swing plane midswing*, right in the middle of one of the most important shots in the U.S. Open. Hitting a 1-iron, an impossible club anyway, in a gusty ocean wind, on a monster of a hole, under all that pressure, he has *total* awareness of a moving golf swing, the effect of the wind on his angles, and he *makes an adjustment*. Remember: his golf swing would move the clubhead somewhere around 120 miles per hour. And still he's able to adjust midswing and hit the shot, and it stops three inches from the cup, 218 yards away. That is self-control to a degree that I just have no words to describe in strong enough terms, from sports to neuroscience to magic. It's just who he was. It came from his character and makeup.

His sense of self-control, ownership, and responsibility were even more evident when he lost. In recent years, looking back, when asked about his greatest shot, he didn't mention that shot or any one shot, but a sequence of holes in 1966 at the British Open. He was standing on the sixteenth tee, he recounted, and said to himself, "OK, Jack, I want a 3–4–4 finish and I think you'll win the Open if you do that." And he did. He finished 3–4–4 and won. How's that for total self-direction, control, execution, and ownership? A few years later, he stood in the exact same place, right among the leaders, and said it again: "OK, Jack, 3–4–4 and you'll win the championship again." Unfortunately, he didn't make the shot that time around, and here is the kicker . . . the main point: as he looked back on that loss, he commented, "I finished 4–5–4 and lost by a shot. *So I had my own destiny in my hands . . . and I just didn't do it*" [emphasis added]. That statement reveals the secret of his greatness. He saw himself as being in control, win or lose.

Listen to the *ownership*, the total realization of who is in control of Jack and his performance: *Jack*. He doesn't offer excuses, such as, "It was windy that day and a gust of wind carried the ball too far on seventeen." Or, "Someone yelled in my backswing." There's no "the dog ate my homework." Instead, we hear total ownership: "I just didn't do it."

I have never seen great performers who felt themselves to be out of control of their own performance, emotions, direction, purpose, decisions, beliefs, choices, or any other human faculties. They don't blame others or external factors. The greats are not like lesser performers, who try to explain away their failure as being somehow caused, forced, or controlled by someone else.

Self-control is a big deal in human performance. Getting better depends upon it. You cannot get better if it's not *you* who has to get better. You are the performer, period. You are the only thing you can control.

In the psychological world, this idea and description of health is called by many names. "Self-efficacy," "agency," and "locus of control" are a few. It is the "perception that one is in control of oneself." If you have a 1-iron in your hand to win the U.S. Open, it's good to realize that it's in *your* hand, not someone else's. If you *do* know it's in your own hand, your mind and body (two parts of Siegel's performance triangle) can adjust it to hit one of the greatest shots in history and win a U.S. Open. If you don't, you'll just continue the swing and then look up to see where it went. Good luck. A lot of people's days and even lives are like that. They look up to "see where it went." The greats in business, sports, or life know that they and only they hold the club. (See my book *Boundaries for Leaders*, HarperCollins, 2013.) And, remembering Siegel's mind as regulator, you can see how a mind that has that kind of self-control can lead to very high performance.

Whether as a business leader, an individual performer, a parent, a spouse, or even as a patient in the health care system, once you realize that—that the 1-iron is in *your* hand—you are on your way to breaking through to the next level. You are 100 percent in control of *your* side of the relationship, *your* levers in the business, *your* input, the training and discipline of *your* kids, and on and on. Self-efficacy is part and parcel of any kind of human performance. Obviously you are not in control of the universe or other people, but you are always in control of yourself.

But this is not a book about self-control. In fact, this isn't even a book just about self. It's a book about the power of the *other*—the power that someone *else, not* you, has in your life of performance, achievement, and well-being. Seems like a contradiction, right? On the one hand, I'm saying *you*'re totally in control of your performance, but on the other, I'm telling you that *other* people have power over your performance too. Which is it? Self-control or the power of others? Anyone confused?

The answer is yes. We all are confused. The reason we're confused is that we see self-control and our individual performance as *totally dependent upon ourselves and what we do,* which is right, and as having nothing to do with anyone else, which is wrong. The truth is that, while our self-control and performance is totally in our control, it derives much of its sustenance from the power of our formative relationships. Yes, others, in the past and the present, help build our capacity for self-control. That is the paradox of performance.

Said another way, how much you perceive yourself as being in control of your life depends in part on how much the most significant people in your life support that ability *and* simultaneously hold you responsible for it. Winners not only perceive themselves as being in control of themselves and their choices, but also they exercise this control every day, and we can see it. They have that incredible sense of ownership, but in part it was built and is sustained by relationship. Here it comes again: Corner Four.

Who doesn't want to be Jack, the kind of performer who breaks through all known limits? This self-control thing sounds pretty good. Who wouldn't want that? But where does self-control come from? Here's the answer: self-control comes from practicing it, building it, and using it *in the context of Corner Four relationships.*

GET A GRIP

As a golfer, psychologist, and performance coach, I have always been interested in Nicklaus's strong sense of being in charge of himself. No matter what anyone else was doing on the golf course, he was focused on what he could control: his own game. I have often thought his will to win was incredible. Where did it come from? Recently, I got another clue.

I was on a trip and channel-surfing late one night when I saw an interview with Jack about his career. The interviewer took him back to his developmental years and the role that his father played in his life and his golf career. He talked about the support of his father, Charlie Nicklaus, who was really into Ohio State sports and very into Jack's golf. As he talked more about his dad's role in his life, you could see the self-control that Jack had been building, exercised in that Corner Four relationship.

He recalled one time when he was a teenager playing in the U.S. Amateur. After a round, his dad asked him about one of his choices on the course—why he had hit a certain shot or chosen a certain club. His dad was questioning him, probably second-guessing him, if you will. At that moment, he looked at him and said, "Dad, . . . it's my game."

It's my game. What an incredible, powerful statement of ownership and self-efficacy. He was defining himself and what he controlled in relation to the person that he was closest to in all of life. (See David Barrett's *Golfing with Dad*, Skyhorse, 2011.) When I saw that clip, it all made sense. Jack's sense of self-control was suffused throughout his being. It was "my game." And he was able to say that directly to the very person who had supported him the most. And because he knew that and owned it, he had a greater sense of self-control than any we have seen or might see for a long time. As I described his approach before, the "1-iron is in *my* hand."

Two things stand out in this exchange: First, Jack was able to express that ownership directly to the person who supported him the most. Second, his dad respected Jack's sense of being in control of his performance. This combination—being in control *and* being supported and respected in your choices even when your other disagrees with them—is one of the most powerful elements of Corner Four relationships. This combination empowers people to achieve their greatest performances, fueled by the other and set free to soar on their own.

Self-control, agency, self-efficacy—all hallmarks of psychological health that undergird performance—are built and supported in relationship to others. The degree to which you are going to soar depends in part upon finding Corner Four partners, who empower your sense of self-control instead of trying to take it away or diminish it somehow. Self-control is built through several functions that others provide:

- Support

- Growth

- Respect

- Accountability

Let's look at how these functions work, beginning with Nicklaus. How did the power of the other (his dad) help him build his own power?

As I noted in the last chapter, human performance requires fuel from relationship. But, the booster engine is not the rocket. The support is not the performance. It is necessary, but not sufficient. Eventually, Jack has to—*you* have to—hit the shot.

To be sure, temperament and genetics explain some of Nicklaus's tremendous achievement, but as we know both from research and from his own story, it was also through his relationship to his father, Charlie Nicklaus, that he developed a sense of ownership and accountability. When Jack said, "Dad, it's my game," that comment came out of their Corner Four relationship, in which his father was his fuel and his support. But his father also respected Jack's sense of ownership and self-control. Charlie Nicklaus supported him from the days of playing junior golf up until the pros. He encouraged him, provided a coach for him, and gave him input, discipline, and much more. But he also gave him something huge that all Corner Four relationships give us: *autonomy and responsibility*. The balance between support and autonomy were there all along. As a psychologist, I can tell you that this balance helped develop the self-control that hit that 1-iron and helped him own the results he got in every other tournament he played.

For instance, on page 107 of *Golfing with Dad*, Jack says this about his father's role when he was deciding whether to continue as an amateur in the spirit of Bobby Jones or to become a professional golfer: "It was clear from our discussions that he was inclined toward my continuing as an amateur, but *he presented his opinions without pressuring me and, at the close of each talk, reminded me that I had to be responsible for my own decisions*" [emphasis added].

The real test of a Corner Four relationship is what happens when you choose a different path than the one your supportive person desires for you. After weighing all the factors, Jack decided to turn pro instead of doing what his dad thought he should do. Instead of being the next Bobby Jones, he became the greatest player in the history of the game. Jack says of his dad, "He is a very unobtrusive rooter." How many people of great talent wish that their bosses, parents, coworkers, spouses, or friends could be unobtrusive rooters, giving them freedom as well as support and not withdrawing when they decide to follow their own paths? That is pure gold.

Even with all of that support and freedom, Nicklaus speaks of his father as in no way just a rubber-stamper. He had his own strong views and opinions and didn't automatically approve of everything that Jack did. As Jack recounted, "He believed in me, supported the things I did, and he was always there for me, *whether I needed a boost or a kick in the rear end*" [emphasis added]. His dad confronted him when needed. He told him the truth, but he did it without violating that basic sense of autonomy that we all need to become our best. Charlie would give input and at the same time respect freedom. "He rarely offered unsolicited advice about my golf game, but he was always there if I asked" (*Golfing with Dad*, 108). What a balance and, in my professional opinion, what a brain builder. The relationship between Jack and Charlie Nicklaus was the very definition of a performance-building Corner Four relationship.

Question: Who do you have who is like that? Who is both giving you support and input, as well as protecting your freedom and control? It might be time to have a conversation with a boss, friend, family member, board member, or someone. After all, what is empowerment if not the freedom to exercise self-control and freedom of choice and performance? Too many times, however, leaders think of empowerment as happy talk, as the quickest path toward getting people to do what they want. They forget that empowerment requires not just freedom to choose, but support from the leader even when times get tough and disagreements crop up. Putting support, real freedom, delegation, and choices all together is a tough challenge for any leader and for most kinds of relationships.

Recently I was discussing this dilemma with a CEO who sometimes finds himself in tense boardroom discussions. One of the most powerful members supports him strongly—until the CEO wants to do something this particular board member disagrees with. If it were a matter of policy, governance, or ethics, obviously, the board member should exert control. Ultimately a board *is* in control. But in the day-to-day running of the company—the CEO's job—the board member ought to be supporting him. He can disagree with him if necessary and even try to persuade him to reconsider a position, but ultimately the board member needs to recognize that it's the CEO's call. He can make that clear and also be perfectly clear that he and the rest of the board will hold the CEO accountable for results, as opposed to withdrawing support at every turn.

Naturally, it can get tricky. Sometimes it's hard to figure out where one's responsibility ends and another's begins. But that is an important aspect of choosing your Corner Four relationships. The best ones engender a constructive dialogue about this very topic— where the line should be drawn—without the threat of withdrawing support if you disagree. Corner Four relationships figure these things out, without one person immediately grabbing the 1-iron out of your hand when things seem to get a little out of control.

THE BALANCE OF FUEL AND FREEDOM

Supporting people and still letting them have control over them-selves builds limitless potential. It is the recipe for greatness. Think about how such a balancing act might play out in various dimen-sions of your life:

What would it mean to you as a leader if your board, your boss, your team, and your investors understood this balance? What if they were there to massively and insanely support you but also to make sure that you retain control in order to do your best job? What if they gave you that freedom and empowered you to take ownership of what you need to control? What if they didn't change or withdraw their emotional tone or support when you make choices, which you think best and are responsible for, if they differ from choices they would have made? For that matter, what if they didn't try to interfere or micromanage you at all? What if delega-tion really meant delegation, that you own it, and that the 1-iron is in *your* hand?

What would it mean to you as a business if every company saw itself in a Corner Four relationship with the field and even with its customers? What if your company asked, "How can I be a fuel-ing support and at the same time make sure that those closest to delivery of the business have all the control and autonomy that they need in order to perform?" That would be powerful. And I have seen it. When it happens, results go through the roof, as well as morale, energy, and entrepreneurial spirit. Horst Schultze, founder of Ritz-Carlton, has stated that his employees are fully empow-ered to satisfy a customer and solve a problem up to $2,000 *without checking with anyone.* They are supported to make choices that help customers without getting approval from above.

What would it mean to you as a spouse if marital partners in general supported each other in their individual pursuits without feeling threatened or left out? What if they gave input when wanted but didn't change their level of support when disagreed with? What if there were mutual respect for different styles and different preferences (aside from loading the dishwasher; there's only one right way to do that!), which instead of conflict and hurt feelings would end in a deeper connection and a stronger foundation?

What would it mean to you as a family . . . ? Oh, wow. Where should we begin? I'm continually amazed at how even extremely high performers' lives are often still controlled in some way by their family-of-origin or in-law relationships. I wish we had some cosmic algorithm that actually revealed how much lost performance comes from people having to continually negotiate the intrusion of family-of-origin conditioning and interference into their businesses, careers, marriages, parenting styles, life choices, and the like. It literally becomes crippling to even some of the most talented people out there. In these situations, even if the adult umbilical cord is providing food, it's charging exorbitant rent. What if it could be otherwise?

What would it mean to you as a friend if your closest friends operated like Jack's father, Charlie? Or like the small group who got me through a difficult situation in my college years? What if they fueled you and supported you just as Jack's dad did, offering help, advice, and resources when needed, rooting for you, and at the same time helping you learn to take more responsibility and ownership for your choices? What if they gave you honest feedback and opinions but let you make your own choices without emotional repercussions?

Sounds pretty great, doesn't it? But keep in mind that Corner Four supporters don't just give support willy-nilly. They support your choices but also hold you responsible for them. Obviously if you're engaging in highly destructive or even illegal behavior, their boundaries may become narrower and stricter. Drug addicts give each other freedom, but without holding each other responsible for destruction. That is not Corner Four support. It won't help you achieve a breakthrough in your life. Corner Four holds people accountable for their choices. In the next chapter, we will see how they foster responsibility.

CHAPTER SEVEN

FREEDOM REQUIRES RESPONSIBILITY

My father was awesome. I loved him with all my heart. He was my mentor, coach, fuel, and supporter in so many ways. He was also big on responsibility and accountability. I am not sure whether this was because, from the age of seven, he was fatherless and had to make his way alone in the world or because of his World War II training and military service as a first sergeant in Europe for four years. He was supportive but could be *very* tough. One of his buddies who served with him in Europe told me the story of my dad disciplining a soldier for some kind of misbehavior by sending him out late at night to "dig a six-by-six," a hole in the ground six feet by six feet by six feet deep—not a fun chore late on a cold night or in the daylight, for that matter. My dad's buddy felt sorry for the guy and sneaked out to help him dig it. My father spotted him out there, came outside, and said, "Well, since you enjoy digging so much, you can do one of your own, right over there!" Ouch . . . but that was my dad.

As far back as I can remember, my father always told me that I was going to go to college if I wanted to. He hadn't been able to go to college, having to drop out of high school to support his family and many siblings. He encouraged me, but with that fueling support, there was also a delineation of responsibility. He would say, "Son, don't worry about college. It is already paid for. That's my job. But your job is to study hard so you can get in. I can't do that for you. But then, after you go, *I'm done*. You'll be on your own." Then with a smile he would add, "You can drop by for a sandwich if you want, but don't expect much more than that." His deal was clear. Support and responsibility. He would support me until I went to college, but after that, I would have to be responsible for my own life. He would give me his support and my freedom, but I was responsible for the choices I'd make.

I will never forget one time when this responsibility arrangement felt like the *last* thing I needed or wanted. I felt I needed help—big-time help—not responsibility.

It was the summer of my freshman year in college, and I was at home in Mississippi for the summer. My college girlfriend was in Texas that summer, going to summer school. We were pretty serious, and her family invited me to spend a week with them vacationing on their ranch in South Texas. I was to pick her up in Austin, and we would drive from there to meet her family.

The reason I was to pick her up in Austin was that her father was the governor of Texas, and she was staying at the governor's mansion that summer. During the school year, I hadn't thought much about that little fact, that her father was the governor. I just liked her a lot for who she was: attractive, smart, fun to be around, and really down-to-earth. You would not have known that she came from "Texas royalty," but she did. Now I had to go meet the family, and it was a little bit disconcerting for a nineteen-year-old kid from Mississippi. I had a few butterflies, but I carried on, drove to Austin, and picked her up.

When I got to Austin, she said that she wanted to take a bunch of her things with us to the ranch, and my little two-seater was too small, so instead we took her car, owned by her father. I offered to drive. So we left on our journey. I pulled out of the governor's mansion in his car and made a turn. Soon I made another one. That's when it happened.

I made an illegal turn, right into oncoming traffic, and we were hit head-on by a big truck. More than an oops, it was a biggee, not a fender bender. We were both OK, but the car was history. Somehow the fact that we had escaped injury did not strike me as a blessing at that moment. All I could think about was that I had just totaled the Texas governor's car, and now I'd be meeting him for the first time: "Hi, I'm your daughter's boyfriend. I just wrecked your car." Let's say the blessings were not in clear view. I wasn't even injured enough to hope for sympathy. I think a part of me wished I were. At least if I were on crutches, he might feel sorry for me.

After dealing with the police (an interesting moment in and of itself when they asked, "Whose car is this?"), I couldn't stop worrying about what to do next. *What was I supposed to do with the fact that I just totaled his car?* Whose insurance company should I call? Who pays? Who is responsible? All I could hear was the old Warren Zevon song going through my head: "Send lawyers, guns, and money. / Dad, get me out of this." *Right,* I thought. *Dad would know what to do.* So I called home.

My father answered, and I told him what had happened. He immediately asked if the two of us were all right, and I assured him that we were both OK, just a little shaken up. He then went silent for a moment. After what seemed like probably longer than it was, he said, "OK, son, let me get this straight: You're on your way to meet your girlfriend's father for the first time, right?"

"Yes sir. That's right," I said.

"And you just totaled his car."

"Right."

"And you're going to be his houseguest for a week."

"Right."

"And he's the governor of Texas."

"Right."

"And the first thing that you have to say to your girlfriend's father, the governor, is that you just totaled his car."

"Right. So, Dad, what do I do? Do I call our insurance? Her insurance? It's not my car. I don't know how to do this or how to take care of it. What am I supposed to do?"

Another silence. Then he said this: "Son, . . . here's what I know. *If you're old enough to get yourself into a situation like this, you're old enough to get yourself out.* But do me a favor. Call me and tell me how you did it. I can't wait to hear!" And he hung up the phone.

If I had had to write a book on what responsibility was at that moment, I wouldn't have known what words to put on the page, but I certainly did know the feeling. I, and only I, was responsible. It was *my* wreck. *My* girlfriend. *My* conversation to have with His Honor. *My* insurance mess to track down and figure out.

The conversation with my father was the equivalent of Charlie Nicklaus saying, "It's not my game, Son; it's yours." This is the flip side of freedom in Corner Four. Not only do Corner Four relationships give us freedom, but also *they require us to take it and own it through responsibility.*

DEALING WITH IT

I once heard former U.S. secretary of state Colin Powell speak at a leadership event; he told a story that captures the balance among freedom, ownership, and responsibility. When he was still national security advisor to President Reagan, his job was to meet with the president in the Oval Office and tell him about all of the trouble spots in the world that he was worried about. While he was explaining those, he said that Reagan kept looking out the window. Then, after a while, Reagan said something like, "Hey, look, they're eating them!"

What? What's he talking about? wondered Powell. He looked out the window. While Powell had been pouring out his woes about world affairs, the president had been watching the squirrels in the yard finding the nuts that he had left for them that morning. Recounting the interaction, Powell basically said that the message from the president was, "It's *your* problem."

Corner Four relationships don't rescue us from hard decisions or responsibility. In business, for example, when your protégé makes a mistake the first time she leads a project and ruffles some team members' feathers, you don't jump in to smooth out the problems her style has caused, but you do encourage this less experienced manager to find a solution and adapt her style.

In dealing with an addict, a Corner Four relationship doesn't mandate trying to physically stop another person from using substances. But it does depend on truth telling, on making clear that if the addict continues down a destructive path, he will have to live with the consequences. The message of a Corner Four relationship is, "I cannot get you out of difficulties created by your choices, but I can require you to be responsible for them."

Certainly leaders can't take a hands-off approach in toto. That's how some big-company CEOs, board members, or other executives get into trouble, asleep at the switch. Think Enron, VW, BP, etc. Obviously, communicating freedom and responsibility is not abrogation of one's own responsibilities.

There is a balance to be sought, holding the delegated one responsible without interrupting or disempowering. This is a very important leveraging aspect of leadership—requiring people to be in charge of what we have put them in charge of, then holding them responsible, with consequences. At Apple such a person is called a DRI, a directly responsible individual. If marketing of a product is broken, that's the person the boss can call. He or she owns it.

I recently had a conversation with a leader I'll call Melissa, who absolutely loves the work that a freelance designer (let's call her Robyn) does for her company. Robyn has become a big contributor to the business as well as a good friend; her work is highly creative and she's very energetic. But there's a problem: Robyn always delivers late. Often very late. And that has not been good for Melissa or her team, as they end up scrambling to make up for Robyn's delays. Melissa had come to the realization on her own that the nature of their relationship needed to change. As much as she loves Robyn's work, she admitted, "Her sense of timing, missing deadlines, and not fulfilling timelines that I'm counting on is not where I want to be. Our company needs someone who sees timeliness as important for our customers. So I am going to have to tell her that I want to use her on the creative side of things, but I am pulling her contract on the execution side. She doesn't execute on a deadline. She's fired from that part of it."

My level of respect for Melissa was already high, but it went up then. Here was a relationship that she cherished and that added much to her business in a certain way. But the nonperformance was not OK and she was going to have to hold Robyn accountable. She was going to be honest about it. And she was. It was a difficult conversation but Robyn didn't shirk responsibility for the pattern of missing deadlines. She owned the problem. She said she had a tendency to want to please too much and that caused her to agree to unrealistic deadlines. She was sorry she'd overpromised and underdelivered, and she also admitted that, honestly, she didn't think she'd be able to do much better if she were allowed to continue with the same expectations and responsibilities.

Now that's what I call a Corner Four relationship. The boss held her responsible, and there were consequences, all in a spirit of being *for* each other. Robyn owned up to her part in the situation without being defensive or taking it personally.

What happened as a result? *Robyn's self-control increased.* Robyn owned the fact that she hadn't taken responsibility for saying yes when she should have said no, and with that realization, she was immediately more in control of herself. The next time she faced a similar situation, she would be able to draw on greater self-awareness and recognize her tendency to promise too much. She'd be able to weigh the consequences of her answer, asking herself, *If I say yes to this, will I be able to do it all?* Thanks to her Corner Four relationship with Melissa and the feedback it provided, Robyn would now be more in charge of her choices and her results. She would be in a position to *choose* to change her behavior if she didn't like the outcomes associated with it. That's self-control.

Think for a moment how this scenario *could* have played out. Suppose Melissa had let Robyn off the hook with a mere scolding. Feelings probably would have been hurt even though the persistent problem of missed deadlines wouldn't have been fixed. Without Corner Four feedback that directly, honestly, and in a caring fashion addressed performance failings, neither person would have benefited, and no learning or growth would have taken place. These kinds of workarounds—which don't really work at all—are all too common. They happen at work, in families, and in friendships, and they end up leaving the relationship in worse condition, filled with unspoken resentments, misunderstandings, and, worst of all, no opportunity for the participants to get better or to realize their potential. (See chapter 11 on Triangulation.)

ACCOUNTABILITY AND EXPECTATIONS

One of the words we hear thrown around the most in any kind of performance circle is *accountable*. Most people mean by it that someone who is accountable is being held responsible for some result, choice, behavior, or the like, and with consequences.

One of the problems we see most often is that accountability conversations are held in negative emotional climates, with toxic outbursts and shaming. We hear "How could you have done that?" and "How could you have let that happen?" (These are really statements, not questions. They mean "You're an idiot!") Accountability has too often meant coming down hard on someone, and we know what that accomplishes: division without learning.

In Corner Four relationships, accountability is different. The responsibility we are discussing in this chapter is not the punitive, shaming, or angry kind, which usually serves the purpose only of giving the disappointed parties a chance to vent their wrath or take care of their feelings.

Corner Four accountability is a commitment to what is best at three levels: (1) both or all the individuals involved, (2) the relationship(s), and (3) the outcomes. There are some big factors in this kind of accountability that keep it from going the route of shame and push it forward to greater performance: The first is the clarity of agreed-upon expectations, which have been communicated and embraced by all. Second, the timing of those expectations is *early* and *continuous*. Before anything substantive is done or not done, everyone knows the expectations and checks in with them during the process. Nothing's worse than finding out you're in trouble when you didn't even know what you were being held accountable for.

Great Corner Four relationships increase responsibility by preventing most surprises. They avoid both "How could you have done that?" and "How was I supposed to know?" Good relationships depend on honest conversations about what each party expects from the other, so the expectations are clearly understood and known. Then the parties stay in touch about those expectations so some big surprise doesn't happen way too late to do anything about it. To fly a plane to a destination, a pilot sets a cruising altitude for the flight plan and checks the altimeter repeatedly so there are no surprises that come too late to fix. Likewise, research in marriage success shows that couples who do well "check in" frequently, sometimes multiple times a day. They stay current. This need is no different for management teams and direct-report relationships as well: stay current, whatever that means and however necessary.

On the other hand, get out of each other's face as well. There's a country-and-western song by Dan Hicks that asks, "How can I miss you when you won't go away?" Micromanaging each other in any kind of relationship makes our entire emotional, relational, and biological system scream, "Get out of my face!" In personal and business relationships, it must be clear to all what the right balance is, what is enough communication to stay connected and what is too much, suffocating.

Corner Four requires clarity in the expectations you have for each other, before it's time to deliver on those expectations, and it also requires staying in touch along the way, at the necessary intervals. Clarity and consistency, monitoring and adjusting, lead to real performance increase.

CONFRONTATION AND FEEDBACK

"Feedback is the breakfast of champions," as Ken Blanchard says. We all know that, at least at some level. But in reality feedback is often hard to give and hard to receive, especially if we're living in Corners One, Two, or Three. In Corner One, there's no feedback. In Corner Two, it makes you feel bad. In Corner Three, it's dishonest, mostly flattery. Here are a few thoughts about feedback to help you get to Corner Four.

First, the science of feedback tells us that it is *crucial* to performance. Without it, you cannot achieve new levels of performance, much less get past a current limit. You must know how you are doing in order to get better. One of my favorite works of performance research is *Flow: The Psychology of Optimal Experience* (Harper & Row, 1990), by Mihaly Csikszentmihalyi, who points out that the best zones of performance occur when there is *immediate* feedback. Rock climbers, for example, get this. They know very quickly how well what they are doing is working—maybe too quickly! Do something that works, you stay on the wall. Do something that doesn't, you feel a quick drop—hopefully not too far.

The brain needs to know how it is doing in order to adjust and do better. If you sway to one side, your inner ear tells you to correct. It provides feedback to you. If you are dropping on the face of a mountain, the sensation of falling tells you to react quickly, reach out, and secure yourself. Your entire system corrects. Don't wait to give feedback until you see someone already falling off a cliff. Give it in the moment, while the climber can still adjust. And don't wait to ask for feedback until you feel the earth sliding away underneath your feet.

Second, for feedback to be helpful, it has to be, well, *helpful*. That's one way Corner Four relationships differ from all others. When you are in Corner Four, you know, first of all, that whoever is giving you feedback is *for* you and *with* you, as stated in the requirements of accountability above. That person is your *ally* and wants you to win. The one giving feedback shares an interest in *your* doing well. I have to believe that when a doctor tells me to take a certain medicine, she is trying to make me well and not trying to kill me, or just bill me. She has a shared interest in my health. She is *for* me.

Sounds good, right? Unfortunately, a lot of so-called feedback never comes at all or doesn't come in a form we can process. If we're operating from Corner One, detached and not emotionally invested in others, we really don't get much feedback that is *for* us. In fact, most of the time in Corner One, we're disengaging from feedback altogether. Isolated and shielded in various ways, we don't let others get close enough to really see what's going on; we don't encourage them to speak freely. We haven't communicated vulnerability to people in a way that would make them want to respond or reach out to help. We are walled off and hidden away.

If we're spending our days and nights in Corner Two, any feedback we do hear just makes us feel bad. I had a painful experience just today (how is that for timing?) with an employee who, I had heard from someone else, was struggling in her relationship with me. She'd told this third party, "I feel like he's on a rampage, just trying to find anything that I do wrong and yell at me for it. I have gotten to the point where I just am trying to do my job and stay out of his way."

Ugh. This was not good news—for her, for our work together, for our firm, and especially for a guy who writes books on how to not have stuff like that happen! I was really surprised, dismayed, and a bit confused.

So I called her and said I wanted to talk. I told her that the other person had told me what she had said and that I wanted to know why she felt that way. I asked, "What have I done to make you feel like I was out to get you?"

She hemmed and hawed a bit at first—probably because she was surprised that I was choosing to address her concerns about our interactions so directly. I reassured her that she was not in trouble, and I shared with her that it saddened me that she was feeling that way. I really wanted to know what was going on for her. So she told me.

I was truly sad that she was feeling like that, and although I didn't feel that I had ever yelled at her or was out to get her, that didn't matter. I told her that I understood what I had done that made her feel that way and asked for her forgiveness. She was right about something, though. Although I hadn't yelled, I had been really bugged about a misstep she had made in not getting something done, and I hadn't let her know in the best of ways, for sure. So I apologized. She said that it helped to talk, and we were able to get to a good place. That place was Corner Four—a place of mutual trust and honesty and accountability. Having moved from Corner Two feelings of hurt and inferiority, she saw things differently now, as did I.

But remember, my confession of having criticized her in a crummy way was not all that we had to talk about. I still needed to communicate the reasons I wasn't happy with her performance. That's the second part of a Corner Four relationship. It can't just be warm and fuzzy feelings, making each other feel good. It has to include constructive, reality-based feedback. I wanted her to feel better, for sure. But I was still unhappy with her performance, no matter how I had bungled communicating my displeasure. So after we got back to Corner Four, I asked, "Can we find a way that, when I let you know that something isn't working for me, it doesn't turn into a bad thing for us? I don't want you to feel like I'm out to get you at all, ever. And at the same time, I need to feel like I can tell you what I need for you to do better. Let's talk about the best way for me to do that."

We had a great conversation, and we're at a different place now. There were two lessons to be learned here. First, I *had* to tell her that she hadn't been the Corner Four person I wanted her to be: on my team and coming directly to me if something's wrong. I wanted her to know that if I do something that's not good for her, *I really need her to come to me and tell me.* (See chapter 11, "The Deadly Triangle of Relationships.") If we don't talk directly with each other, we've drifted out of Corner Four into a disconnected, depressing, or shallow relationship. She acknowledged that she hadn't talked to me directly as she should have, and she promised to do that next time I screwed up.

However, I couldn't let the performance issue that was bothering me go by without talking about that, too. By not doing what I needed done, she *hadn't* lived up to our performance standards. I needed her to do better than that. If we were going to truly be in Corner Four, I had to tell her the truth and know that she could hear it. I wasn't out to get her and didn't want to make her feel bad, but I couldn't be unhappy with how she is failing me, and be stuck with it, frustrated because I couldn't tell her without her feeling attacked. I need her to perform, and when she doesn't, I need to be able to tell her and fix the problem. People in Corner Four relationships care, are honest, and fix problems.

Corner Four demands all three: *caring, honesty, and results*— caring enough about someone to not be hurtful in how we say things, the honesty to say them directly, and a focus on behavior change and better results. Remember these three accountability aspects: the individuals, the relationship, and the outcomes.

Business, marriage, friendships, teams, culture, health, and life likewise demand all three. We must be open and trained to receive the feedback, listen to it, and take it in so as to develop self-control that leads to great performance. You will *never* get to the next level if you can't embrace feedback about your performance at the current level. Executive coach Marshall Goldsmith puts it aptly in the title of one of his books: *What Got You Here Won't Get You There*. Getting to the *next* level happens only when you are open to feedback and know how to use it. Moreover, it happens only when you're actually *getting* feedback, when someone is telling you the truth. We can't change what we do not know we need to change.

Corner One is getting no feedback at all. Corner Two is getting it without caring and probably without accuracy, as the other person always has a standard that is somehow unhelpful or unreachable. In Corner Three, anything but feel-good backslapping or flattery is off-limits. Only Corner Four provides both caring and reality in the form of usable, actionable information. When we get that, it helps build self-control and the realization that we *can* do better. We *are* in control of outcomes.

Let's look a little more deeply into several factors that make Corner Four feedback work.

THE BRAIN AND FEEDBACK

Have you ever been yelled at, put down, or scolded when someone was ostensibly helping you get better at something? Remember how you felt? Of course you do: horrible—ashamed, afraid, anxious, sad, angry, and/or closed off. What stood out most to you in that moment—the feedback itself, or how you were feeling about it, the other person, or yourself? No doubt you were much more in touch with *how* you were feeling—awful—than with *what* was being said. The actual issue, what was truly important, was no longer what you were focused on.

There's a reason for that. In highly charged emotional moments, the part of your brain that gets tapped for action is called the amygdala. Chemicals get released there that interfere with learning. Threat of any kind can trigger a fight-or-flight reaction, which is not focused at all on learning, only on protecting oneself. Hence the "checked-out" expression on a teenager's face while being scolded. In those moments, a dose of adrenaline floods our brains, producing anxiety, and we literally go blank. Whenever we're in fight-or-flight mode, we can't absorb feedback and improve our self-control and learning. To learn and grow, we have to embrace the feedback. In my book *Integrity* (HarperCollins, 2006), I talked about the importance to leaders of "embracing negative realities." It's essential. But think about this: whom would you *rather* embrace—someone who's yelling at you or someone who's smiling?

Research has shown that the brain responds best to a ratio of five positive feedback messages for every negative message. In business research, the best ratio is actually six to one. The highest performers get an almost six-to-one ratio of positive to negative feedback, but the lowest performers' mix is almost the opposite, a ratio of one to three. The people who perform best are hearing six positives for every negative, while the worst performers are getting three times more negatives than positives. For sure the negative is needed—we need to know how to get better—but in the right ratio and tone for the brain to use it.

Consider how this balance plays out in sports, for instance. A great golfer like Nicklaus needs feedback from the muscles in his arm if he is swinging the club off path. They shouldn't "feel right" when he swings it the wrong way. But what if he experienced *piercing pain in his forearm* whenever he swung the club in a certain way? Without even realizing it after a while, he'd probably start avoiding that position and flinching every time he didn't. His performance would get worse. He'd be afraid to move. If we're experiencing destructive pain, physical or emotional, we can't deal with much more than the pain. This is how your brain works in response to the emotional pain of uncaring feedback or a threat to security. As the research shows us, apparently the brain needs a lot of love, safety, and good feelings to be able to handle negative inputs and use them. If I'm going to own my game, I can't be in a defensive stance, ready to flinch. That's important to remember when you're on the receiving end of feedback, but it's also critical if you're the one giving it.

When I called my dad to tell him about the car accident, he didn't yell at me. In fact, he seemed kind of amused at my mess once he realized no one had been hurt. But he gave me feedback that let me know that it was "my game." He didn't rescue me from it, and the emotional interaction didn't get in the way of my seeing that it was my problem. He didn't say, "You freakin' idiot! That's how you're going to go meet your girlfriend's parents? I knew we should have never let you go on this trip." If he had responded that way, what kind of response would that have engendered in me? I probably would've been thinking what a jerk I had for a father or what an idiot I was for having a wreck. But because he didn't do that, I was thinking about the *real* problems: a wreck and a bad start to a relationship with my girlfriend's father. That required growth, and my father had produced an opportunity for it by the nature of the feedback he'd given me.

Research into brain circuitry shows that new capacities grow when we have to grapple with a problem ourselves instead of hearing someone tell us how to fix it or watching someone fix it for us. We remember about 10 to 20 percent of what we read or hear or see, but 80 percent of what we experience in such a learning process. When someone provides feedback that leaves us in shape to grapple with the problem ourselves, we learn.

Research has also shown that we are able to retain more focus, have better concentration, think more clearly, and process information better when we aren't experiencing negative emotions. They just get in the way. The higher-performing parts of the brain get sidelined when we're experiencing negative emotions, and the lower, more reactive parts kick in.

USABLE AND ACTIONABLE

A woman told me, "I have an issue with my boyfriend."

"What is it?" I asked.

"I want him to connect with me more," she said. "I don't feel that connected to him."

"That's not good," I said. "What have you done about it?"

"I told him."

"Told him what?"

"I told him I wanted him to connect with me more."

"You did *what*? You actually said that to a guy? That you wanted him to 'connect more'?"

"Yes. What's wrong with that?" she asked, taken off guard.

"Well, how did it work?" I asked.

"It didn't. He didn't do anything different."

"Well, what was he supposed to do different?" I asked her.

"Connect," she said.

"Well . . . how? How is he supposed to do that?" I asked. "Connection is a result of doing some specific things. How is he supposed to act on that 'connect with me more' request? He probably has no clue how to do that. I bet his eyes glazed over."

"So what should I have done? I thought I was trying to express my needs to him in a vulnerable and good way."

"I get that. It sounds like you did. The problem is that when someone is not doing something, it's probably because they don't know how. So to just tell them about the result you want doesn't help them. What if you said, 'I'd like it if after work we could get together a few evenings a week and take a walk . . . undistracted, and just catch up and share what happened during the day, or how each other is doing.' I bet if he cares he'd say, 'Sure, I'd love to.'"

The difference, I explained, is that this suggestion is something actionable, a specific something that you'd like him to do or stop doing. This is something he can do something about. He can control making time to go for a walk, but he can't control whether you are feeling "connected."

She nodded. In this interaction, I had also done the same thing with her. I hadn't told her to just be "different" somehow or not to talk to him that way. I gave her some specific feedback.

CONSEQUENCES AND PAIN

Corner Four relationships don't rescue us. They hold us responsible for our performance. There are standards and there are consequences. Few things are worse for the culture of a team than rewarding or overlooking poor performance. It clearly tells the underachiever, "What you're doing is good enough," and tells the others, "Your efforts toward excellence, your care, and your diligence have no value."

Jim Blanchard, the former lead director of the board of AT&T and CEO of Synovus Financial for thirty-five years, was heralded by *Fortune* in 1999 for building the "#1 Place to Work in America." Synovus was one of only a few companies inducted into the Fortune Hall of Fame. I asked him why his company rose to the top of these rankings. He explained that he's always seen the culture as being just as important as the business plan.

Leading up to this recognition, many important things happened. The leaders established the values and norms of behavior that the company would embody—to care for, develop, respect, appreciate, empower, and help employees—and they were very serious about holding people accountable when they didn't live up to those cultural values. Blanchard said two things that stood out to me. One was that the leadership team made a vow that they wouldn't give anyone a boss they wouldn't work for themselves. The other was that they wouldn't tolerate anyone being mistreated, bullied, or dealt with in any way that was not respectful and caring. He also told all of his employees that if they were mistreated by a boss, they should try to work it out with him or her first, but if they couldn't get resolution, they could come directly to him. He told them that if he didn't deliver on this commitment, they had no reason to ever believe anything else he told them.

Why was this arrangement significant? It made very clear and specific what behaviors were expected. It made clear that it was everyone's responsibility to build a healthy culture with the values they'd agreed to enforce. Those executives and supervisors who didn't accept these standards or couldn't perform in that manner were simply not suited for the job at Synovus. Over the next two years, about two hundred leaders departed Synovus. Some were regular retirees. Some tried, were coached and counseled, but couldn't fit the cultural requirements. Some tried and were successful in the transition. Some were simply asked to leave. Some left voluntarily because they chose to seek another environment. But the net-net was a dramatic improvement in quality of leadership and the workplace environment. That's the mark of a culture of true responsibility and accountability. It paid off.

First, it got all personnel in control of themselves. Someone who was treating others badly was given a choice: improve or leave for somewhere more suited to that approach. Such clarity leads to greater self-control. Some exercised it; others chose not to. Once everyone understands the standards to be met and sees what happens when they aren't, a positive feedback loop drives more learning and growth and produces new levels of achievement.

There is no freedom without responsibility, and that is generally taken only if there are consequences for *not* taking it. A standard without consequences is a fantasy, a wish, or a suggestion, not a standard. And consequences that involve no pain or loss aren't consequences at all. Real ones mean that if I don't meet the standard, I lose something important to me. Otherwise, we drift.

In a Corner Four connection, the standards must be enforced. They create a protective barrier that keeps the system, the relationship, or the culture healthy. If you allow bad behavior, the entire system suffers. As Jim Blanchard told me, "People who violate the values really need to be somewhere else. If not, they really ruin what you are trying to accomplish."

Unfortunately, we've all seen it happen. A teacher who allows one student to constantly disrupt the class. The boss who allows one team member to make the culture divisive or difficult. The family who allows one person to ruin holiday gatherings. Facing reality can be painful and difficult, but the consequences of not confronting it are always far worse.

PRACTICE AND FEEDBACK

Here is one of the greatest motivators I can think of for getting feedback: myelination. Myelination is the process by which your brain increases its ability and speed to send signals down the circuitry by growing myelin, a specialized fatty tissue, around the nerve fibers. It speeds up the processor. The more you have, the better the wiring can conduct signals. Put simply, the more we practice, the more we repeat something, the more myelination happens, and the wiring for that behavior gets stronger. Practice makes perfect. Or as Malcolm Gladwell states in his book *Outliers* (Little, Brown, 2008), ten thousand hours of *deliberate* practice is the key to mastery. While research disputes the number, there is no doubt about the value of practice. The brain needs it.

As magical and important as myelination is, it alone doesn't ensure that we'll learn and grow through repetition. It's an agnostic process; it does its thing whether we're creating productive or destructive experiences. It can't upgrade the wiring for some experiences and ignore others.

That's why the combination of feedback *and* deliberate practice is so important. It's not just a matter of swinging the golf club for ten thousand hours; it's doing so with feedback from coaches, from your results, and from exposure to different techniques (and don't forget talent). Repetition creates wiring, but it's constructive feedback that creates the positive patterns we want to repeat and reinforce. If we're doing something that's not helpful to us or others, we need to know *quickly—before it becomes a pattern*. That's why when my daughters were learning to play golf, I worked with them from day one so they wouldn't ingrain bad patterns that would be very difficult to overcome later. Only feedback can do that.

Find Corner Four feedback that can set you up for long-term growth and success. Once you know what is helpful and good, you can pay attention to that behavior even more. That attunement creates new brain wiring as well. Feedback causes a lot of good things to happen, besides saving us from forming poor performance patterns in the first place. Better yet, it can guide us to repeat what's helpful over and over again until it becomes part of who we are.

FREEDOM, RESPONSIBILITY, AND LOVE

At the time of this writing, my two daughters are thirteen and fourteen years old. They are incredible. I could not have dreamt how much fun they would be. I have heard many people remark, "Oh, going into the teen years. Sorry!" Or something pessimistic like that. But that's not my experience.

I was traveling not long ago and getting a haircut. The guy cutting my hair commented, "I have a teenage girl too."

"Oh, great! How old is she?" I asked.

"She's sixteen," he said.

"So . . . are you having fun?" I asked.

"Nope. Not yet," he said somewhat seriously.

Sorry, I thought.

I know it can be a tumultuous time, and I know it won't all be a bed of roses. Ask me ten years from now how it went, and pray for me in the meantime. I have no illusions about doing this perfectly, but I'm still optimistic. They're great girls.

However, partly because I'm a psychologist and partly because of everyone's words of caution, I decided that it was probably time for a formal talk with them. I told them one of my favorite formulas: freedom = responsibility = love. Here is a summary of what I said:

"Girls, you're becoming teenagers. It is an exciting time. One of the reasons is that you will be getting more and more independent. That means that you get to do a lot more stuff on your own, and you're going to want the freedom to do those things. So I want you to understand something.

"My deepest desire is to give you as much freedom as you want. I have no plans to control you on some short leash. In fact, I want the opposite. I want you to be in control of yourself and have as much freedom as you can. So here is how it works. It's a formula. The amount of freedom that you will have will be equal to the amount of responsibility that you take when you have it, and that responsibility should be measured by love. The choices you make, that you will be responsible for, are to be loving. They must be good for others and for yourself. Your choices should not hurt anyone in any way—you or anyone else. That is your guide to responsibility. If you are responsible in that way, guided by love, you will get more and more freedom. As much as you want, as long as you follow the formula: freedom = responsibility = love.

"If you are not responsible with the freedom that I give you, if you do things that are not good for yourself or others, things that are not loving, then your freedom will be limited to that same degree. It is totally up to you how much freedom you will get in the teen years. Show me that you can be responsible with it, and you will get it. That will make my life and yours a lot of fun!"

I am sure we are headed for some testing of those limits, but if I can make sure that I'm a Corner Four dad—supporting them, offering them feedback, giving them freedom, and requiring *responsibility with it*—that's the best I can do.

I believe in this formula. I want it to prevail for all of us in every relationship we have and in every business as well. Think of what's possible when every person has the fuel, the freedom, and the responsibility to rise to greater and greater heights.

CHAPTER EIGHT

DEFANGING THE BEAST

In chapter 5, I shared a story about one of my darkest moments in business. I had blown it significantly, and one of my hero-mentors called me in the midst of my failure. His kindness and empathy made me feel less alone during that time. But that Corner Four connection also helped me confront something else: the very real and deathly grip of failure. *My* failure. I truly knew that things had gone badly because of *me*. I had been the one who had made the stupid mistake. I had been the one who had thought I was doing well but didn't have the wherewithal to know that I wasn't.

How was I supposed to deal with the feeling of being such a *loser*? The "fangs" of the beast that was slaying me were feelings of judgment, failure, guilt, shame, and condemnation for missing the standard against which I was judging myself. I had really, really blown it, and winners don't blow it this badly.

Or do they?

What truly released me to be able to move forward and ultimately overcome the failure were the words, "Well, we've all been there." But why? Why were these five words the key that helped me not only recover, but get even better?

DOWNWARD SPIRALS

As a psychologist I can tell you that when we are in a negative critical state, the brain, the mind, the spirit, and the soul are all in a downturn. Our brains experience chemical states that create a toxic ocean of self-recrimination. The brain is not doing its best thinking, problem solving, or a host of other capacities that you need to win. The cycle continues, pulling us deeper and deeper into a depression that saps energy and our capacity to think differently. But breaking the pattern requires more than a shoulder to cry on. *We need to take the fangs out of failure.* That's what my friend's statement—"We've all been there"—did. It normalized failure.

That someone as successful and admirable as my friend had been sitting exactly where I now found myself helped me confront the unrealistic standards I was using to condemn my performance. With his help, I didn't have to fear failure anymore; I could see that never failing wasn't the standard I should shoot for; the goal was to continue to go after things, to seek out opportunities, not to avoid them for fear of failure. In other words, failing should be viewed as just another way of putting yourself on the path to winning. As he said, they (the winners) "have all been there."

For as long as humans have been around, we have struggled with an age-old issue: the dynamic tension between how things ought to be and how they are. Where I want to be versus where I am. Here is the bottom line: *high performers resolve that tension in very, very different ways than the people they consistently outperform.* In what way? Basically this: they are fueled by the possibility of better instead of defeated by it. When confronted with failure, they are inspired to keep trying; they don't judge themselves for missing the mark. Their desire and drive are not minimized or crushed by failing. That is the difference in their performance. Again, though, it's not just a matter of individual willpower. Research confirms that it is "otherpower," if you will, that helps us to experience failure as a means for improvement, as an opportunity for *better*. Think about it. In one conversation, my entire psychological, physiological, emotional, motivational, and intellectual orientation got turned around. My mentor had reframed the goal as something that was alive—something that I could still aim for, not a one-and-done, life-or-death moment. And through the interaction with him and others, that frame came to live inside of me and be my own.

Of course, I already understood that intellectually. We all do, but when the fangs have us in their grip, it feels so real; it's hard to see failure as a temporary state of affairs. We need the "other's" help to internalize it.

Indeed, neuroscience research shows that a disapproving facial expression, one that indicates a negative evaluation, signals your brain that you have done something socially undesirable and that your relationships might be in danger. Rather than focusing on possible solutions, we become overwhelmed by fears of rejection, insecurity, and failure. Obviously, when we're mired in these kinds of feelings, we're unlikely to be able to notice, let alone address, objective gaps in performance. (See Lisa J. Burklund, Naomi I. Eisenberger, and Matthew D. Lieberman, "The Face of Rejection: Rejection Sensitivity Moderates Dorsal Anterior Cingulate Activity to Disapproving Facial Expressions," PubMed, www.ncbi.nlm.nih.gov/pubmed/18461157.) The fangs of the beast are in you, and you're more concerned with your relational safety than with solving the problem. When your brain detects that an important function in creativity and performance could be better, you want it thinking about how to get better, not how to avoid being rejected, feeling like a failure, or getting yelled at. That's why it's crucial to have an outside perspective from someone who is for us in our Corner Four. Like a veteran pilot who knows how to guide a plane full of passengers safely through turbulent air, our Corner Four relationships show us how to push beyond feelings of despair and helplessness toward new possibilities. That is what my friend did for me.

In everything we do, whether as a business leader, a parent, an amateur athlete, or a spouse—two realities exist simultaneously: where we *are* at any given moment, and where we *want to be*. The space to be negotiated between these two states is the *gap*. We can't avoid the gap, but we can decide how we'll approach it—or as they say in London Underground stations, how we'll *mind* it. Does it become motivating or defeating? Do we use it as a guide for how to improve or as a judge of how much we're failing? Consider how one of the highest performers in the film industry navigates the distance between these two realities.

THE STORY OF PIXAR

With megahits such as *Finding Nemo*, *Toy Story*, and *Monsters, Inc.*, Pixar, under the leadership of CEO Ed Catmull, has pioneered a form of storytelling that is both an artistic and a commercial success. It's no surprise that Pixar attracts the world's top talent, but it may be a surprise to learn that it has also built a highly collaborative, highly sophisticated Corner Four relational culture, which can be extremely difficult when artistic personalities are involved. Part of that culture is built on the premise that failure is more than OK; it's welcomed. In my words, Catmull and his colleagues have created a Corner Four culture by "defanging the beast of failure."

As Catmull says in his book, *Creativity, Inc.*, "What makes Pixar so special is that we acknowledge we will always have problems, many of them hidden from our view; that we work so hard to uncover these problems, even if doing so means making ourselves uncomfortable; and that, when we come across a problem, we marshal all of our energies to solve it. This, more than any elaborated party or turreted work station, is why I love coming to work in the morning. It is what motivates me and gives me a definite sense of mission."

Pixar doesn't police mistakes, but it does try to root out negative attitudes and counterproductive structures and behaviors. Catmull and his colleagues recognize that creativity requires a culture of safety and that Pixar has to be intentional in creating such a culture. "I've spent nearly forty years thinking about how to help smart, ambitious people work effectively with one another. The way I see it, my job as a manager is to create a fertile environment, keep it healthy, and watch for the things that undermine it."

The "fertile" culture Catmull describes makes it safe for people to not always be perfect and to not always get it right, but it also provides for processes and structures that ultimately ensure extraordinary results. And here's where it gets tricky. Healthy cultures need to make it safe for people, but they also need to make sure people don't get too comfortable. Healthy cultures embrace people where they are but they also nudge them and sometimes even *push* them to get better.

Catmull describes creating certain rules that preserve psychological safety and inspire the team to get better. He normalizes the process by acknowledging that, in the early stages, "all of our movies suck. . . . I make a point of repeating it often, and I choose that phrasing because saying it in a softer way fails to convey how bad the first versions of our films really are." Then he addresses the gap—going from "suck to not-suck." By doing so, he helps his talented, driven team see that there is a process for closing the gap, a path that will take them from where they are at the moment to where they want to go.

How did he create this kind of relational safety? First, he focused on creating a peer-to-peer culture with no bosses. He got rid of all signs of hierarchy at creative meetings, replacing conference tables and place cards with comfy chairs to reinforce the sense that everyone is equal and on the same level. Second, he insisted that everyone have a vested interest in the film's success. Above all else, the film had to be right. It wasn't about whether individuals looked good or appeared smarter than everyone else. It wasn't about individuals winning; it was about making the best movie possible.

Finally, Catmull created a give-and-take culture of reciprocity. He required that his team "give and listen to good notes," or

feedback. I love the emphasis here on "give and listen to"—not holding back on the giving but also being able to receive feedback. Both
sides are important. His focus on listening means *receptivity* on the
other end. While the sender mustn't fire bullets, the receiver can't be
defensive, either. In Corner Four relationships, we need to be open
to receive, but we need to be sent "receivable" feedback that is not
injurious. As the neuroscience research shows, we cannot absorb
feedback when we're caught in the fangs of fear and failure.

I recently had an experience in an executive team off-site for
a technology company where this dilemma was front and center.
A very bright junior member of the team got some feedback from
one of the senior members about a plan he had written. The senior
member just didn't like the product. Rightly, she said so, following
one of the key values this team had established for itself.

The recipient of this feedback immediately bristled and got defensive, and the meeting's tone changed. You could feel it. Even
though they continued to discuss the plan, there was a cold tension in a previously lively meeting. The recipient's body language
and tone gave him away. Finally, I stopped the discussion and said,
"Hold on. Let's talk about what's happening here. This is not OK."

"What do you mean?" he said.

"You have totally disengaged, pulled away, and you sound very
different, like you're really miffed or something. I don't feel like
we're really talking about things anymore, even though we are still
talking. You seem like something is really wrong. What happened?"

"Ok . . . you want to know? I'll tell you. She is so critical of
everything I do, and *so* difficult to work with," he said. "I just find
it better to stop trying. Ever since I joined this team, she has been
shooting me down."

"Like how?" I asked. That sounded terrible. Maybe I didn't know her as well as I thought I did and she was a monster in other settings. It happens.

For the sake of the team, I knew we needed to work on this dynamic right away. As Catmull emphasizes, creative cultures must "overcome the unseen forces that stand in the way." So we dived into it.

The junior member of the team went on to describe how he felt—that there was no way to win with her, that she was always so "harsh." The rest of the team and I just listened. I could see that there was more going on here than just his relationship with her. While she was very direct and her feedback was often served without cookies and milk, her intentions were good. She could be forceful and even a bit aggressive at times, but she was honest and really in it for the team. But that's not what he'd heard.

"I didn't hear what she said in that way at all," I said.

"What do you mean?" he asked.

"I just think she was giving you her opinion. She does that to me all the time—much more brutally than I just heard her do with you." I looked at her and she blushed. "But it seems when she does it to you," I continued, "it hurts instead of feeling helpful."

I pointed out that I'd had this same experience with him recently. He'd felt that I wasn't respecting him when I'd pushed back on some of his comments. I reassured him that I didn't want him to feel bad but that the team needed to find a way to give him feedback without it feeling so personally hurtful.

As we talked more, he revealed that he had never worked in a culture like this, one where real, honest feedback was freely shared but where no one constantly felt threatened. At the places where he had worked before, everyone tried to be nice, but often they weren't honest. He was still having trouble believing that this team's values were for real, not just lip service. What's more, he was able to see now that some of the resistance and defensiveness he'd been expressing stemmed from his own tendency to take well-intentioned comments as put-downs.

This was an important insight for him, because to truly benefit from Corner Four relationships, we must realize that this inner dialogue can interfere with giving and taking feedback. We may hear harsh words when the intention is to offer a helpful critique. This often happens when someone has had previous wounding experience with a boss or in another relationship that colors later interactions, those voices and scripts still playing in the background. Some people have spent their whole lives submerged in Corner Three flattery. No one has ever told them that not every thought or idea they have is special, so when someone offers feedback, they experience it as harsh or as a sign of not being respected. We often filter current relationships through the cloudy lens of the past.

At this particular off-site, meanwhile, we continued working through these issues and made some progress in building a Corner Four connection. The junior executive copped to his need to work on hearing things differently, being honest at the moment when something doesn't feel good, and asking the other person what they really mean. That was huge. I applauded him.

Likewise, the senior member of the team took some steps toward becoming a stronger Corner Four person herself. I had turned to her at one point and said, "And by the way, he's not making all of this up, you know. I know you don't mean it in a mean way, but you could watch your tone at times, and it might help." She laughed and said, "For sure. Please tell me when I'm being that way." That's real Corner Four movement in making the beast your friend instead of foe.

As Catmull points out, we all need to be able to tell each other that "the film sucks" but know that it isn't personal and we all want the same thing, to make it better. Corner Four is a both/and place. *We need to say it well, and we need to hear it well*, even when it's not said as well as it could be. That's a start, but we also need to build the capacity to say it better, to present our feedback forthrightly but kindly. When we all begin to do that more often, we grow the same capacity in others. Goodness knows, we'd all benefit from a little more kindness in the world. We *need* kindness to grow. We need a lot of it, and if we get a lot of it, we are better able to absorb those moments when kindness fails. For example, if you have given me kind, helpful feedback a thousand times before, then when you have a bad day and slam a door, I'll be more likely to feel empathy and concern for you rather than assuming the worst and shutting you out. That forbearance increases the level of safety in our connection and makes it even easier for us to give and get feedback— not just to recover from a momentary blip, but to get altogether better and deliver that next blockbuster we're all shooting for.

Fortunately, there are a few things we can do to help this process along. Central to this effort is the intentional and proactive creation of two things:

1. Standards for how we communicate that we want something to be better.

2. Monitoring how well that communication is being done.

WAYS AND MEANS

We need some operating standards, values, or behavioral rules to help good feedback thrive. At Pixar, for example, they all assume that there'll always be problems and they'll always be addressing them. What a great standard!—as opposed to no-problems-allowed cultures that make it dangerous for anyone to speak up, let alone grow into doing their best work. Another Pixar standard is peer-based collaboration. Said another way, *ideas have no rank or position.*

This is an awesome standard that makes you free to disagree with a boss if you think his idea is no good. Also, when he tells you he doesn't like your idea, you don't have to see it as a reprimand or fear for your job or next promotion. Pixar also promoted a "for" culture—in that feedback was viewed as something offered in service of a greater good (i.e., making the best film). Every piece of feedback was in the service of that interest, to help everyone win. Moreover, Pixar placed equal emphasis on giving and getting feedback. That was part of everyone's job— not just to give it but to receive it in a way that would serve the greater good.

These are great rules for Corner Four teams and organizations. In my work with executive teams, I often find that results suffer when the team's ability to give and receive feedback is broken. This is often more of the problem than the strategy or the execution plan itself. It's easier to blame failures on a poor product or some aspect of the operation that failed, but too often the problem starts further upstream—with a failure to communicate in general but specifically with a failure to give and receive feedback in a way that is forward-looking and focused on getting better and neither blames nor covers up weak links on the team.

That's why I encourage teams to develop a few simple rules and communication standards. I encourage the team to share past experiences when feedback has helped them get better or set them back, so they can come up with an approach that will speak to where they are today and where they want to go—with the goal of minding that gap.

One team I worked with came up with this guiding paragraph for their rules of engagement: "We engage in respectful, collaborative, *timely*, and complete dialogue. We clearly and directly convey ideas and share our points of view, while maintaining openness to different perspectives. We listen to understand and respectfully question to achieve clarity, in both message and mutual expectations. We openly discuss critical issues and deliver difficult messages with care. We commit to not leaving important things unsaid, and we avoid saying them to someone other than the person who should hear them." (See my book *Boundaries for Leaders*, Harper-Collins, 2013.)

Others have done it in other ways. Here are a few examples:

- Focus on the problem, not the person.

- Let's love every idea for five minutes (or some amount of time—forty-five seconds?).

- Say it with respect, but say it all.

- Listen and think about it before negating or disagreeing.

- No zingers or over-the-line personal attacks.

- No back-channeling or side conversations.

The right rules for Corner Four relationships, whether personal or professional, depend on the circumstances. But no matter what standards you establish, recognize that you're determining, on the one hand, whether your messages will be heard—at all, with respect, kindness, and honesty—and on the other, whether you'll be able to *take* respectful, kind, and honest feedback to reach beyond your current limits.

That's why it's helpful to build a mechanism into your Corner Four relationships to help you give each other feedback on how you give feedback and whether you're living up to the feedback standards you've established. You have to be able to *monitor how you monitor* these relationships.

I recently worked with a CEO and his team as they were experiencing some difficulties in team dynamics. The team had become divided on an important strategic topic, three members having formed a coalition of sorts against another two members. The CEO said that he was always feeling caught in the middle. He didn't want to feel that way, and he finally stood up and said, "No more. This is not going to happen on my watch, and if you guys can't begin to act respectfully toward each other, you'll have to find somewhere else to do that."

The CEO had let the squabbling members know that if they chose to continue to act the way they were, he'd have to boot them from the team. In the spirit of a real Corner Four relationship, he'd given them the freedom to choose how they wanted to behave, but he'd also let them know that there would be consequences to their actions. Fortunately, they were able to take this feedback at face value, as a sign that the CEO was *for* them and *with* them, and the discussion produced a clever new standard to help the team stay true to its values. We called it the flag.

A football referee throws a flag when a rule has been broken, and this team decided it would use a similar monitoring system to ensure that everyone played fairly. If any team member felt that the conversation had veered into sarcasm or that some of their activities had become cliquish or divisive or generally interfered with the group's values or goals, then that member could throw out a yellow flag to stop play. (They actually got some yellow flags to keep on the conference table during their meetings.) Every member of the team was given permission to stop the game in order to correct an infraction.

Similarly, so-called process checks are helpful in other meetings of teams. They can also be helpful with couples or in family meetings. It's useful to take a moment and ask questions such as:

- How are we doing in trying to help each other get better?

- How is our feedback going? Are we giving enough? How could I make my feedback even more useful to you?

- How could I receive this feedback in a more open manner?

Alan Mulally, the legendary CEO who was brought in to turn around Ford Motor Company, was known for having twelve clear principles for working together. Many industry experts have credited this clarity of vision and behavior, and the team's ability to bring that into a failing culture and make it real, as one of the reasons Ford was able to come back from its near-death experience. According to some observers, it was a common practice for Mulally to begin meetings by reading aloud this list of principles, and then at the end of the meeting, he'd revisit them, asking, "How did we do?"

He is a great example of both things we are talking about: having a standard and monitoring adherence to it. This kind of process check is essential for changing any behavior, especially the behavior that changes all other behavior—the ability to work together with others to improve. When our methods of getting better get better, we get better. Work on getting better for sure, but work on your methods of getting better, as well. You'll be glad you did.

CHAPTER NINE

THE RIGHT KIND OF PUSH

Imagine that you're at the bottom of a mountain, wanting to get to the top. You have finally gotten your courage up, and you've put a lot of time and effort into creating a plan to get there. And so you begin. You take a few steps, but then you slip and fall, landing just about where you started. At that very moment, a ninja at the top of the mountain rolls a boulder down toward you. Another throws a poisonous spear, just missing you. You wipe your brow and ponder whether to get up and try once more, but then you realize that the penalty for slipping and falling again is this kind of punishment. All you can focus on at that moment is how to avoid the onslaught of boulders and spears that will come your way if you falter again. You give it another try, halfheartedly this time, but still you make no progress, and still the stones and spears come at you.

That's where I was that night until the beast was defanged. But after my friend defanged it, failure was no longer attacking me because of his understanding and normalizing it. It made falling a normal part of climbing the mountain. I was no longer being attacked by poisoned spears or boulders for not doing well. But I *still was not out of the woods*. . . . What now?

If you continue doing the same thing, you're going to get the same results. Even if you're *not* being attacked by faceless enemies, your own clumsy efforts bring you back to zero. You're no longer getting attacked, but you haven't gotten better, either. You try, but you get only to the same level. No matter what you do, you're stuck.

You want to go higher, but you keep hitting the same kinds of obstacles over and over again; you keep getting tripped up by your own mistakes. Even if the beast of failure has been defanged, you're still left to your own devices, destined to repeat what you have tried before.

You're hitting your limit. You may not be feeling bad anymore, but you're also not getting to the next level of growth you desire. There is still something that has to change. What should you do?

OPEN WIDE

In other writings, I've referred to the second law of thermodynamics from physics as one of my favorite metaphors for explaining how human performance works. Basically, the law states that in any system, there is a limited amount of energy, and over time this energy becomes less useful and more chaotic. As much as the system tries to keep order and make progress, inevitably the energy, and thus the quality of the system, grows more disordered. That decay of order and energy is called entropy. Despite one's best efforts, the system is running down, getting worse instead of better. So it goes with human performance.

The same with businesses too. A management team continues to work a plan that has been successful in the past but keeps hitting a wall that is explained away by various factors or excuses. This goes on indefinitely, until it's impossible to deny that business results have flattened out or started to decline.

It happens all the time with individuals, too. A golfer practices and practices, yet still can't get his handicap below a certain number. A couple plans date nights to rekindle intimacy yet continues to argue about the same issues. A leader follows best practices of his own making, but the slam-dunk strategies that worked in the past don't raise the score.

If you've read my other books, then you'll know that there are two ingredients essential for breaking out of the cycle of decline: *new sources of energy and intelligence.*

In business, we have a term for this kind of person: the turn-around artist. That's what Alan Mulally was when he brought Ford back from the brink. He injected new energy and contributed new intelligence, infusing the culture with a new set of practices and values that reversed entropy. In personal relationships, these new sources of energy and intelligence might come from a therapist, a wise friend, a coach, a pastor, or a support group.

Still, *you have to be willing to open yourself*—your team, your business, your family—to receiving this influx of energy and intelligence. As in most other situations, you get to choose.

CONSIDER THE SOURCE

Let's say that you accept my premise that you're going to need something from outside yourself to get where you want to go. You've defeated the crippling bite of failure, but you realize that not feeling bad is not the same as accomplishing your goals. Corner Four relationships possess specific ingredients that help people move uphill, so you need to surround yourself with Corner Four people. What should you look for in a Corner Four relationship that will help you surpass current, known limits?

I should make perfectly clear that I'm not suggesting that you jettison all of your dysfunctional or non-growth-producing friends, family members, or coworkers. Goodness knows, our lives are made interesting, fun, and sometimes slightly wacky by all types of people. We are blessed to have them in the mix. But you do have to realize one thing: *they're not all likely to provide you with new energy or intelligence.* Headaches, belly laughs, and unforgettable experiences, yes; juice, maybe not. So you have to make sure that you are sourcing energy through multiple channels and looking, in particular, for the kinds of relationships that add energy to the system. What do those look like?

STRETCH

Commander Rorke Denver is a former Navy SEAL who saw a lot of combat in a thirteen-year career in that elite fighting force.

He frequently speaks at leadership events, inspiring people and sharing his principles and experiences as a SEAL. At an event we did together last year with six thousand people in attendance, Commander Denver asked audience members to stand and raise their hands toward the sky as high as they possibly could. After the sea of arms and hands were pointed high all over the arena, he paused. Then he said, "OK, give me two more inches!" You could see all those people raise their hands two inches more than they thought they could. Six thousand people thought their arms were as high as they could go, but when he challenged them, they quickly realized they had *more*. Twelve thousand arms went higher! It was an amazing sight. With just one suggestion, they'd pushed farther than they'd thought possible.

The premise of this quick exercise is that we have more potential than we know, and that the only way to know how far you can go is to try—but that requires a little helpful nudging from a Corner Four relationship. A push. . . . a stretch.

Frequently, we don't have a clue about the abilities and assets we possess. They have never been pointed out to us. That's what the right kind of Corner Four relationship does: it spots a hidden asset you possess and shows you how to access it. The best kinds of others balance a couple of factors in setting stretch targets:

1. They will push you to go farther than you've gone in the past, encouraging you to develop new skills in order to reach the goal.

2. However, they will not stretch you to a point that will overwhelm you or take you backward.

The best leaders, coaches, and friends do *both* of those things. They push you past where you have been or thought you could go, but not so far that you can't recover. *They stretch but don't injure.*

As Mihaly Csikszentmihalyi describes it, peak performance occurs when we are constantly challenged but not too much for our newly acquired skills. If we are put into challenging situations that surpass our newly acquired skill set and push us *too far*, we'll slip out of the sweet spot where learning and fulfillment—flow— occur. As we acquire new skills (and confidence), we can step up to more challenging goals, but the trick is to get the balance right between the amount of stretch and level of skill required to succeed.

The right amount of stretch boosts our skills and our confidence; the wrong amount can send us back to the fangs of failure. (Think of it this way: if you decide to do a marathon for the first time, you gradually build mileage over the course of many months to be ready for race day. You don't announce your decision and immediately run 26.2 miles all in one day if your previous limit was 2.) On the other hand, if you are not challenged *enough*, you risk falling into what Csikszentmihalyi calls the boredom quadrant. I call it disengagement. It awaits someone used to running 2 miles who is asked to run 2 or even only 2.2. It is not enough of a challenge.

Great Corner Four relationships push us upward at all times. They will not let us stay where we are, lest we plateau, get bored, disengage, or go looking for another relationship that keeps us awake (say, in Corner Three). As I described earlier, humans are connection-seeking systems, but *arousal-seeking* ones, as well. If we get bored and disengaged, we can't help but search for something to reenergize us, even if the stimulant comes in the form of an illicit affair or other risk-taking behavior. It is due to lack of engagement that many relationships fail; if one partner isn't bringing new energy and intelligence into the relationship, the other person may grow disinterested in investing more intimacy in the relationship. That can lead to all sorts of destructive behaviors.

The same is true in business. Job satisfaction depends on more than financial compensation. After financial needs are met, people seek out positions that offer other things, one of which is the chance to develop new skills and stretch toward higher positions of challenge and growth. They want to grow.

Although top talents want exposure to opportunities that will test their potential, if you constantly put people in a position of high stress that's too big a stretch, they're likely to become discouraged, overwhelmed, and anxious. Eventually (or quickly) they will leave. Leaders must inject just the right amount of tension into the system to motivate their people, but not so much that their people shut down. Stretch them and they'll move toward the goal. Stretch them too much, and like rubber bands, they'll snap.

We know from neuroscience and education research that learning takes place and performance improves with higher states of arousal, but only up to a point, beyond which performance falls off. This relationship is called the Yerkes-Dodson law. As anyone who has ever given a speech or a presentation knows, butterflies before one takes the stage often help *boost* the performance, but *not* if that energy turns into stage fright of panic disorder proportions.

Typically, the more cognitively intense the skills required are, the less arousal can be tolerated. Think of trying to learn calculus while someone is screaming at you. But no matter what kind of task, the fact is, *we need to be stimulated from an outside source in order to keep our system healthy and thriving.* Indeed, research on goal-setting shows that when we are asked to meet very high goals, ones that are difficult but specific, people thrive. We're built to be challenged to grow. This is why the healthiest kids come from environments that do two things: encourage them with warmth and give them high expectations.

I encourage you to ask yourself a series of questions about whether you have access to the right kinds of connections to help you get to the next level:

- Am I being appropriately *pushed* to be better, to be more?

- What specifically am I being *challenged* to do better?

- What specifically am I being *challenged* to do that is more than I'm doing now?

- Am I being pushed *past* my comfort zone?

- When I resist or struggle, how are these feelings *addressed*? Do others remain firm in my need to grow?

10X CHALLENGES

Sometimes the stretching we need is what Jim Collins refers to as "big hairy audacious goals (BHAGs)." To reach these goals would surpass anything we have ever done before. Not just incremental steps, but goals that change everything, taking us ten times farther than we ever thought possible.

Great visionaries push people to these seriously mind-blowing achievements. When President Kennedy said in a special joint session of Congress in 1961 that he wanted the United States to send an American to the moon safely by the end of that decade, that was a BHAG. When Google's cofounder Larry Page started toying with the idea of self-driving cars while still a graduate student, long before the technology was developed, he was in BHAG territory. His stretch was not to build just a *better* car, but to find an entirely *different* way of getting from here to there. Where did he get that kind of thinking? Or the thinking that created Google? From sitting on a stump in the woods being visited by a muse?

No. He got it from the *Other*.

It was a summer training program in college called Leader-Shape that he attended. The program taught him a new way to think: to have, as he put it, a "healthy disregard for the impossible." The teachers and coaches he met through that program encouraged him to pursue his dreams, as big as they might become, which he certainly did. As he recounted in a commencement speech about those huge, impossible dreams, at the University of Michigan in 2009, one of them was to "**download the whole web, and just keep the links.**"

OMG! From that dream, Google was born. But what if he had never met the people in LeaderShape, the *Others* who contributed new energy and intelligence to his system? What if he'd had only others who encouraged him to follow the well-trodden path of traditional expectations, just do a little better?

In that same speech, Page recalled that when he was way out there in scaryland, starting Google by maxing out credit cards to buy hard drives, he felt like a "sidewalk worm during a rainstorm."

He said the lesson he learned and wanted to pass on was this: "What is the one-sentence summary of how you change the world? *Always work hard on something uncomfortably exciting*" (Larry Page, University of Michigan Commencement Address, May 2009).

"Uncomfortably exciting." Sounds exactly like the sweet spot of peak performance that other researchers have described—that delicate dance of increasing your challenge while testing new skills. These kinds of peak flow experiences, when we are really moving, growing, and learning, create intense focus, bringing all of our cognitive resources online and into active engagement. The brain has something to marshal its greatest resources around, and it comes alive doing that.

A friend of mine who has built a real-estate empire puts it like this: "If, at some point each day, I sit and think about what I'm trying to pull off and don't get a total panic attack, then I know I'm not stretching myself and doing a hard enough deal." He too is describing this uncomfortably exciting zone. He thrives on it, and it has made him zillions.

But this kind of stretching is not just for real-estate moguls or Google founders. We all know people who have made outrageous dreams a reality, with a boost from the other. Think of an inner-city kid who was told by her teacher that she could go to college and become a doctor. Or the stay-at-home mom who was encouraged by a neighbor to start her own business. Or the young associate who is tapped by the founder to launch a new product. Give the brain a *specific*, but *BIG* problem to solve, and it will surprise you. Give people a chance and the tools to grow, and they will shine. *But only if the problem is big enough.* And then only if the process is fueled, monitored, and sustained by the other.

ONE STEP AT A TIME:
A PLAN OF STAIRS

An absolutely critical role that others play in helping us achieve our goals is to help us create a realistic plan for getting there. As you think about the others in your life, ask yourself these questions:

- Do they help me set small, achievable *goals* that are aligned with the big ones I desire?

- Do they help me monitor *progress* in ways that are helpful and specific?

- Do they *value* the small steps I'm taking, or do they only praise "home runs"?

- Do they *celebrate* small wins?

- Are they or have they been on a *get-better* path that was incremental and step-by-step to a very large goal? Do they understand that process?

- Do they *compare* me to the ideal examples only?

- Do they help me identify multiple *options* for achieving my goals, or is it their way or the highway?

All too often in business you run into an executive who values only big wins. Consequently, people can feel devalued or even get pushed into taking risks that exceed their skills and experience. Great leaders and performers consistently take moments of celebration to mark *small* wins. They relish *little* victories because they see them as part of a long-term process.

Good coaches have been doing this for ages. Now we know from brain science why. *Our neural wiring and circuitry are built in the context of encouragement and positive emotions.* Research on goal setting offers a number of important lessons when it comes to building Corner Four challenges. We know, for instance, that the goals we set for ourselves and others must be *challenging* enough to activate our energy and our brains, but they also must be *realistic* and *achievable*.

It's also important that the difficulties of achieving these goals be spelled out and addressed. Blind positive thinking, the research shows us, does not work, because when obliviously positive thinkers encounter difficulties, they get discouraged and bottom out. Corner Four people not only help us believe that we *can* get there, but they also help us see that it is really, really going to be a *lot of work*, with lots of obstacles. They make the difficulty normal. They will be there to cheer us on, but they will also be there to talk us through difficult patches.

We also know from research, particularly the work of psychologist Carol Dweck, that those who possess a "growth mind-set" rather than a "fixed mind-set" are more likely to be able to achieve goals and improve. People with a growth mind-set see talent as something that can be developed and improved, not as an innate, fixed asset that doesn't change over time. The way I like to think of this is what researchers have termed mastery goals. You are focused on trying to get better and master something, rather than thinking that you're either good at it or you aren't. In fact, researcher Heidi Grant Halvorson actually calls them "get-better" goals, a great way to think about them.

In a get-better mind-set, we're always trying to improve, asking ourselves, *OK, what could I do a little better? What can I learn for next time?* This mind-set should not be limited to post-failure moments, either, but maintained in the midst of difficulties, as well.

People who are committed to mastery don't freak out (as much) when they hit an obstacle. They reassess and then get going again, thinking they can get better. That's why you want someone in your Corner Four who possesses a similar mentality. We've all had far too much experience with the opposite: parents, friends, siblings, or bosses who, once they get a certain view of who you are, become fixed on that picture of you; they measure all of your subsequent actions against that standard, no matter how out-of-date it becomes. No matter what you do, no matter how you improve, their view doesn't change. If that's how they see you, then they're not going to be very helpful to you, not committed to or engaged with your progress. They believe that's just the way you are, period.

But there is another group of people who look at the world through the growth mind-set. *They believe that people can grow and change.* They have a developmental bias in the way that they see other people—not as they are now but as they can be. I can't tell you how many times I hear people say, "Well, you know, people really don't change." Unless I'm getting hired to change their minds, it's almost not worth the work of the argument. They just believe that.

But it is absolutely not true. Science has shown that we can change. We do change. We do get better, but *we tend to do it alongside people who believe that too and who are committed to helping us.*

I have written about my dad earlier in the book. I shared how much I loved him and how great he was in so many ways in my life. He helped me learn a lot of skills. He taught me how to play golf, hunt, fish, and think about business and lots of other parts of life. I felt his encouragement in the activities that he participated in with me.

I say that to contrast it with one of his favorite sayings, which I absolutely *hated* when I was growing up but never knew why until I became a psychologist. It was a phrase he would use when I was discouraged that something I wanted to tackle or accomplish seemed too big. If I talked about the difficulty involved, he would say, "Well, that's no hill for a climber."

That phrase always made my heart drop. I would feel discouraged and de-energized. And alone. I realize he said it to encourage me, but it had the opposite effect. I never really understood why until I began to study goal research and the power of the other, the role of encouragement, and how we overcome obstacles. When he said that, he wasn't saying, "You can get good enough to do that." He was saying, "You should already be able to do that. You're a climber."

In addition, he tended to use the phrase only when the challenge involved a goal he wasn't directly involved in helping me master. I might express some worry, and his reply would be, "That's no problem. That's no hill for a climber." His response left me alone in my thinking. In his mind, I was already there; it was just a matter of doing it right. In my mind, I knew that was really far from it. I wished that, even if he weren't involved in those parts of my life, such as academics, he would have said something more "get-better" oriented. It would have helped. He might have said, "That sounds hard. It's going to take some work. How can I help?" Or, "Where can you get some help?"

Don't worry. I'm not parent-bashing here. I'm deeply grateful for many things both of my parents did for me and pray I do as well with my own kids. But understanding this aspect of research really helped to explain those feelings. When we head out of our comfort zone, we need improvement-oriented supporters in our corner.

Goal researcher Heidi Grant Halvorson contrasts a mastery approach with the approach she calls the be-good goal orientation. (See her book *Succeed: How We Can Reach Our Goals*, Hudson Street Press/Penguin, 2011.) People who see goals in this less-than-helpful way adopt a performance orientation basically to show that they're "good enough," and it ends up either validating them if they reach it; or showing that they "don't have it," if they don't. As a result, they're always trying to prove that they're talented, capable, smart or whatever each time they pursue a goal. It's a test of their self-worth, if you will. (This explained to me why I sometimes used to feel relief, rather than fulfillment, in the accomplishment of a goal.)

With that kind of orientation, if you don't do very well, it is much more of a disaster than for those with a mastery approach. The "be-good" group tends to see any mistakes or failings as a sign that they aren't worthy; the "be-better" group sees failure as a chance to learn and try again.

When my dad would tell me "That's no hill for a climber," he was putting me in the category of good climbers, and then the performance was going to prove or disprove that assessment, which didn't serve improvement or learning in any way. (I get anxiety just thinking about it.) In contrast, Halvorson points out another aspect of the "get-better" orientation: it leads people to ask for more help, which leads to improvement and busting through limits. People with this orientation ask for help more than the be-gooders, because asking for help proves to be-gooders that they're not as good or smart as they want to be, and others might see that as well. I remember almost having to convince my dad that he was wrong, I was *not* a climber, it *was* going to be hard, and I needed some help.

At the other end of the spectrum, the best Corner Four people treat each scene in your journey as important, and they make sure you see it that way too. Each scene is a step, and they don't expect you to know how to do it well before you do it. They don't look for perfection, but they do notice and celebrate small improvements. This creates an atmosphere in which growth can happen, and with the other factors like fuel, ownership, accountability, and feedback, it does.

One example of how this approach works is Weight Watchers, which focuses on a known-to-be-stuck population (people who are overweight, have tried to lose weight, and can't). They help participants break down their goals into smaller *steps*, which are then *monitored* and *structured* for success. Each day, participants are encouraged to be in *control* of their *own* choices. They get a certain number of points that they can use to create meals. As long as they stay within their daily limit, they're good to go. Failure one day is just another *step* in the process. Along the way, they keep in touch with *someone* when they need help. Additionally, they *meet* for *group weigh-ins* and *share strategies* and *encouragement* with one another. They give and take, continuing forward and upward . . . or in their case, downward (notice the factors here that we have seen the research validating).

Remember: the Corner Four relationships that are going to help you the most are the ones that push you to take small steps consistent with your vision and your stretch goals. I know this firsthand, as an author. In fact, without this process, I would never have written my first book, nor this one, nor the thirty-something books in between. I cannot take the credit for selling millions of books. I owe 99 percent of the success to my Corner Four relationships, which have literally made it happen. (I just did what they told me.) Here is one example of how they did it in the beginning, to help me get past my limits.

My very first job as a clinician was in a leadership consulting firm in Newport Beach, California, which is where I fell in love with the study of leadership. After working with CEOs and high performers and their organizations for several years, I had built several models of personal and leadership growth that I was using. It was just the way my mind works: as I see issues that leaders need to address for their own growth and for their organizations, I love to build models that capture the conceptual dynamics and the implementation methods that prove most effective. It kind of comes naturally. But I was *way* too disorganized in those years to ever write a book. *Way.*

One day, when I was doing a leadership training session with an organization that had about fifty thousand people around the world whom they wanted to develop, the leader asked me, "Is this stuff written down anywhere?"

"What stuff?" I asked.

"This model you just put up on the board. We could scale this and use it all over the world, in transferable concepts," she said.

"Uh, it's right here . . . on the board," I said, a bit sheepishly.

"Well, we need to get it really written down," she said. "We need a book."

That's how it began, but not without a lot more help. You see, I was nowhere near able to even *conceive* of writing a book. Writing patient notes in hospital charts or a Happy Birthday card to a friend was about the extent of my writing abilities. Talk about a stretch goal! The client might as well have asked me to play for the Lakers. Besides, back then I was the least structured, scheduled, disciplined person you could have known. I did a lot and worked a lot, but the daily discipline of writing and writing and writing, along with doing all of my other work, seemed like a crazy fantasy, but because I loved the material and the vision, I said yes. I would do it. But I neither had a clue as to how, nor the ability to pull it off.

So, I began to think about how to go about it. I collected notes and thoughts for a little while, but I wasn't getting anywhere. Stuck. Meanwhile, the organizational client kept asking for a book. I knew what I wanted to say; that part was clear. The hard part was doing something I'd never done before, organizing all of that stuff into a book. It just wasn't happening. To put it mildly, I was stuck. Luckily, my Corner Four client intervened, because her organization needed a book with the model in it.

So get this: my client, for whom *I* was a consultant, hired *another* consultant to help *me* write a book. Talk about the tail wagging the dog! But it made sense to me, since I was in way over my head in the writers pool. All I had was the content, so they opened up the system, brought in new intelligence and energy, and we began.

My writing consultant and I set up a regular structure of meetings. I was given homework to do in between, and then we would meet and take the next step in putting it all together. Over the course of several months, I developed a pretty structured outline and organized all of my constructs, ideas, and illustrations as a basis from which to begin typing words.

I was working full-time and had no free time to write during the week (something that is still true!), so I committed myself to a plan. Every Friday at 5:30 p.m. when I got off of work, I would go home and write during all my waking hours until Monday morning, when I'd go back to work. The only break I'd get would be going out to dinner with someone on Saturday night, either a friend or date. That was the regimen.

I stuck to it, and six months later, *I had a book*. Stretch goal achieved, through the power of the Other! The book got written not only because my client initially pushed me to the stretch goal, but also, more to the point here, because the consultant played *an ongoing role in pushing me to incremental, get-better, get-more-written goals*. The combination of the big goal *and* the little steps, empowered by relationship and accountability, got me there. This Corner Four relationship provided something I didn't have myself: the know-how and the structure to put my ideas into a scalable form to help others. For that, I will always be grateful. Took a village.

Funny side note: I'm on the board of an organization that has a lot of intellectual property that the leaders want their founding president to put into a book. They had been trying to get him to do it for several years, and he was just not getting it done. Stuck. He had all the content, but the structured process of writing a book was not in his makeup. Being the visionary, people-oriented type, he was never going to get that done. Finally, the board took a stand, as they saw it as critical to the organization. They wanted it done, period. They were getting bugged with him at the lack of progress over years, and had finally had it.

We were in a board meeting one day, and they said, "How can we get him to write this book? How in the world do you get a person who has never written a book to get it done? We *need* it. We *have* to solve this."

I smiled. "I think I know how," I said. I volunteered to help him get it done. Now he is near completion on a project that had sat there stuck for years. That's the thing about Corner Four. It tends to get passed on. One day this guy will help someone else write a book.

PUTTING IT TOGETHER

I like to think of the process and the dynamics of Corner Four relationships as a healthy, well-rounded diet that contains the essential ingredients we've discussed:

- Connection that fuels

- Connection that builds self-control

- Connection that builds ownership and responsibility

- Connection that makes learning and failure safe

- Connection that stretches to big visions and goals

- Connection that names and empowers small, get-better steps

Here is another question for you: How do you *stay* on this well-balanced diet for the rest of your life? How often do you eat? One meal a day? Two? Three? Once a year? Let's go to the next principle of Corner Four.

CHAPTER TEN

BRINGING THE OUTSIDE IN

So now you know how utterly clueless I was in my twenties when I embarked on my first book project. It was only due to the power of the other that I was able to stretch toward my goal. All of the elements of a Corner Four relationship were present: my admission of my need for help (that part was easy, as I was inept at writing a book and desperate); fuel from an outside source in the form of inspiration, encouragement, structure, and process; and a sense of ownership and freedom backed by accountability and consequences in the form of deadlines and deliverables to my client, a stretch goal with push and "get better" steps. I can promise you I would have never, ever been able to write a book at that time if the power of the other had not been brought to the table. Never.

And today, twenty-five years later, I'm *still* using that same consultant to help me write my books. Well, not really. I mean, yes *and* no. In fact, I've never worked with that consultant again. And yet, I have, each time I've written a book.

What I'm trying to get at is one of the truly magical things that Corner Four relationships bring us. It's called *internalization*. It's like some sort of superfood that keeps you healthy and charged up long after your first bite.

INTERNALIZATION

What makes Corner Four relationships so powerful is that they don't end even after they end. The lessons we learn, the phrases that motivate us, are ours to keep forever. Psychologists refer to this process as **internalization**. It's bringing what was on the outside inside. It sounds a little mysterious, and it is. It's a gradual process by which the patterns, tones, fueling, and cadences of our relationships become embedded in the internal structure of our minds, our psyche.

Internalization starts at birth, when we begin to adopt a self-soothing system in infancy. Think of what's happening when a mother calms a crying baby—how quickly the infant moves from a state of upset and frustration to contentment and safety. Soothing is one of the powers of the other. But, after a few hours, that comfort has disappeared and is needed again. It has not yet been internalized.

Initially, we need a caretaker to provide that comfort, but over time, with the right kinds of relationships, we develop the capacity within ourselves to provide that comfort and safety. That's what I mean by self-soothing. The resource that was once on the outside came inside, a part of the baby's very own self—internalized.

This process continues at all stages of human development: our experiences with others are continually being taken in and encoded into our operating system. In this way, the power of these relationships is multiplied, ideally providing us with a strong foundation for interacting with the larger world. At first, a parent cautions, "No, don't touch the stove! Don't pull the cat's tail." Gradually that "no" voice begins to live inside the head until one day, approaching the curb, the child hesitates, slows down, stops, and turns to look for Mom or Dad to give permission to walk into the street. Just like self-soothing, the voice of "no" needs time and practice to be internalized. As the external parent's no is repeated over and over, with a positive emotional tone and needed consequences, there comes to exist inside of the toddler a new psychic *structure*, an internal "no" muscle, a capacity to say "no" from the inside, even automatically.

That's what happened to me, as well. The book-writing know-how that was once on the outside came to live inside, so even though I never worked with the consultant again, he has helped me with every book since, his knowledge of structure being internalized in my brain. Every time I've walked up to the curb and been tempted to dash into Procrastination Street, his voice has been inside, giving me the structure to stay on track. I have used the basics of that system and structured process for every book I've written since.

The developmental lesson here is that the external voices, those relationships and interactions with the other that have fueled, limited, corrected, and encouraged the child to take and be in control of each next step have been internalized and are now available for her to use *on her own* to negotiate the world for the rest of her life. She literally now hears those voices in her own head. You might be able to relate to this if you have ever been to a psychologist who said something like, "You have some old tapes or voices in your head that you need to deal with." They weren't kidding and that wasn't psychobabble. That was science. Former relationships and experiences do live inside us and do continue to affect us. Consider one research study, cited in Halvorson's book *Succeed* (Kindle loc. 873–80), that demonstrates the power of the other—in this case, fathers. While performing difficult math tasks, the students' fathers' names were subliminally flashed on a screen. The internalized father affected performance, without the student even knowing it:

> *Psychologist James Shah interviewed college students to determine how much each student's father valued high achievement. He found that when the students were subliminally (unconsciously) exposed to their own father's name before completing a set of difficult problems, those students who associated Dad with the goal of high achievement worked harder and performed better. Also, the closer the relationship with Dad, the stronger the effects.*
>
> *But when it was over, they had* no idea *that they had been trying particularly hard. The goal of achieving was triggered by unconscious thoughts of their fathers and was pursued completely without awareness.*

Interestingly, unconsciously thinking about a loved
one who does not *approve of a goal can also* inhibit
its pursuit—you are less likely to want to get drunk or
leave all the dishes in the sink if your unconscious mind
is envisioning your mother's wagging finger or disap-
pointed sigh.

Halvorson also describes interesting research showing that for
"rebellious" persons, a subliminal reminder of an achievement-
loving dad triggers *less* effort and *worse* performance! (Of course,
any teacher or employer who's ever tried to get work out of someone with an authority problem knew this already.)

Stop and think about these findings for a minute. This is the
power that another person can have on our performance, even
when that person is not anywhere near us. But they are: *they live in
our heads*. Dad is still there! (As you ponder that, some of you are
grateful, and some of you, not so much, right?)

Don't worry . . . the good news is that the process continues
throughout our lives. New relationships provide *new* voices and lessons that get internalized, sometimes updating or even replacing
previous ones. Indeed, new positive voices from our Corner Four
connections often help us see why it's prudent to discard some of
those old negative internalizations. That's another reason to try to
spend more time in Corner Four. Your new Corner Four voices can
be internalized and overcome the old. One way or another, positive
or negative, our performance is affected by all these voices, from
the present and the past. If you truly want to get beyond a current
limit, your most important task is to run to Corner Four and get
the right voices in your head.

IT'S NOT ABOUT YOU

A CEO of a multi-billion-dollar public company turned sixty and started preparing a succession plan. He was concerned about how he'd be able to move on to a new stage in his life while ensuring that the company would continue to thrive and operate without his being there to guide it. He told me his worry: "How can I move on and have the company continue the same, *as if I'm there*? I feel that it all still rises and falls with me, and my team still acts as though it does. I want to be totally out, gone from the team, and I want them to not miss a beat."

Bingo! I thought. That's exactly the task at hand for leaders, parents, and others in supportive roles. How do we ensure that our lessons, experiences, and values get passed along without our having to be there each and every moment? That's the magic of internalization.

I'm reminded of a conversation I had with someone who wanted to know how I was feeling about the fact that my teenage daughter would soon be dating. He asked, "So, are you going to make sure you interview each date before she goes out and make sure he's OK?" I couldn't help but feel that this person was really asking whether or not I would be up to his standards of a "worthy" dad.

I didn't take the bait but asked instead, "So, what if I'm out of town that night?"

"Good question. Would you let her go out if you were out of town and couldn't interview the date?" he asked.

I paused for a second and then turned the tables. "Let me ask *you* a question. Are you concerned that I'll let my daughter go out with someone I don't approve of? Are you wanting to make sure that I make sure she doesn't go out with destructive guys who aren't good for her?"

"Exactly," he said. "I want to know that you are going to protect her."

"Then my answer is this: *absolutely*! I will interview each and every one of those guys, and make sure that they're OK for her to go out with. Even if I'm out of town."

"What? Wait. How will you do that?"

My friend seemed confused, so I explained: "By having the kind of relationship with my daughter in which my values have been strongly internalized in her head. Every guy will be evaluated by *her own thinking* about whether or not he's OK, and hopefully, her thinking will include mine. I want her to hear my voice in her head asking, 'So is he really OK? Or is he an irresponsible selfish kid who won't be good for you?'"

I went on to explain why I didn't need to be there in person before every date. I said it was important for my daughter to internalize the values of a father who loves her and wants the best for her. I said she needs to make those her own, because if the values protecting her from bad guys live in *her* head, then they will be protecting her whenever she leaves the house, long after my interview.

"In your system," I said, "my protection ends at the front door when they leave. In my system, it goes all the way to the prom and after. I want to *trust* her, not *control* her. And yes, if I do happen to be in town, I'll be on the front porch in my rocking chair, with my overalls and shotgun, and I'll meet the boy and ask him about himself." That is also part of the internalization. . . . Put my camouflage and Waffle House T-shirt on and meet the boy!

What was once outside comes inside. When someone on a date or at a party offers her drugs or sex, I want him to run squarely into me and hear "Go away!" *even if I'm not there.* She will tell him.

Back to the conversation I had with the soon-to-be-retired CEO. I agreed with him, that it was important for the company to continue with the same values, and the solution I offered freed him to move on. I reminded him that, in the first several decades of this company, his employees had worked with him day in, day out. They'd had the chance to watch how he thought, to understand what he valued, and to adapt and learn from him every day. His values and his visions had been internalized, instilled into a culture that would be there even when he was gone. Our work, I told him, was to proactively make sure that the very "DNA" that made the company great—a lot of it in his voice and values—would be passed on to new employees at *every* level.

Together we would focus on that internalization. He needed to make it a strategic initiative. We would develop a structured plan to make sure that the company's cultural DNA was driven down throughout the organization and that it would be there, in each meeting, even when he was no longer walking the halls. And as we would do it through his team, it would even further develop them.

Our task was to figure out which parts of the organization still depended on his presence, especially at different levels of the organization, and accelerate the internalization process so that dependency was eliminated. One of the most important tasks I work on with high-level executives who just can't let go of certain things is to turn what they know into a process, a repeatable formula or system that they can teach and coach others to use. It always surprises people how much they can actually let go of if they know how to get it out of their own heads and into the heads of other people. They find they're not as indispensable as they thought, and they are also freed to take on the kinds of challenging goals that the company needs in order to grow and thrive.

CHANGING THE CHANNEL

Early in life, we don't get to choose what kinds of relationships we're exposed to or which of those voices start replaying in our heads. But as we mature and recognize that we might be hitting a limit, we have the opportunity to choose what kinds of relationships we want to participate in, what kinds of voices to internalize in order to stretch further and reach higher. Fortunately, neuroscience research shows that we can *rewire our brains*—literally. Just because you had voices that diminished you doesn't mean you can't get new ones. Your brain is available for downloads and updates to its software, but just like your cell phone, *it has to be plugged into a good network, with unlimited data and no viruses.*

One of my pet peeves is that many (not all) of the psychological methods and techniques popularized and even professionalized in the last few decades disregard internalization altogether, even though it is the basis for all growth. Consider these popular phrases:

- Change your thinking, change your life!

- You can't love anyone else until you love yourself!

- Find the "power within."

- Overcome fear with positive "self-talk."

- Positive thinking: the key to success.

- You have the power!

Here's the problem. None of these slogans recognizes the power of the "R-word": *relationship*. Yet all the research supports the view that the Big R is the key to the Big G: *growth*. Don't get me wrong. There is truth in each of these methodologies. For example, we know that internal destructive messages, "self-talk," can be a real source of pain and can limit performance in every area of life, and it must be replaced with positive self-talk. And we *do* indeed have personal power, the agency or self-efficacy discussed earlier. But what limits these approaches is their assumption that we can just *do* those things. It is *as if* we can each improve as a closed system, *as if* it all comes down to our own thinking and choosing, *as if* we can just do it, even when we have never been able to do it before. *As if!* The slogan I find most infuriating is the one about how "we can't love others until we love ourselves." When your car is out of gas, you have to visit a gas station. You can't just talk yourself into having more fuel.

It comes back to a failure to thrive, which I discussed in chapter 1. Even if our physical needs are taken care of, we can't develop the capacity to love and bond with others unless we've been cared for and loved by someone else. There's that "Other" again. If you've never had the caring and regulating relationships whereby those abilities are internalized, then you won't be able to love others well either. Empty people can't love others very selflessly. They're operating out of a vacuum of insecurities and needs. You've seen what happens when someone who has never had a warm, giving relationship enters into marriage, where those skills are required. It doesn't work, and just telling them to "love themselves first" won't work either.

Those who have never internalized love often seek and function in relationships in immature, self-soothing ways. Then as soon as the relationship fails them in some way, they don't have the internal relational equipment or internal capacity to work through that failure, and the relationship breaks down. At that point, when they're struggling to make the relationship work, telling them to "just love yourself" is not merely unhelpful; it's the wrong message entirely. Instead, they must find some others who will support and love them and teach them *how* to love others, mentoring them, just as good parenting would have done. Others are going to have to give them something so they will then have something to give. *Love does not begin with oneself.* Love begins by receiving love, internalizing it, and then giving it away to others—paying it forward.

So hear me here. I'm saying that the capacity to build deep connections comes first of all from *outside* ourselves; then we internalize it neurologically, biologically, psychologically, and otherwise, through good connections, modeling, and the like. We learn to soothe and regulate our emotions when an external soothing system is internalized. We learn to challenge ourselves when someone pushes us past our perceived limits, and then we learn to do that for ourselves. We learn to think differently and to think about our thinking by having someone observe us and get us to observe ourselves. The wiring, patterns, and other components of the very equipment to do all of that is in large part *first* internalized from the outside.

This is the essence of the best training and performance development. So-called self-improvement—the process of getting better—is really a relational enterprise, not a "self" enterprise. An interesting word derivation comes into play here, noted by Csikszentmihalyi regarding the role of competition in improving performance. When individuals seek growth and self-improvement in the *competitive* arena, it's not the winning itself that motivates them, but rather the presence of the *other* in the competition. The word *compete* comes from the Late Latin verb *competere*, "to seek together." It is the "together" aspect that drives us. I love that! As he points out in *Flow* (Kindle loc. 1570–76):

> *What each person seeks is to actualize her potential, and this task is made easier* when others force us to do our best *[emphasis added]. Of course, competition improves experience only as long as attention is focused primarily on the activity itself. If extrinsic goals—such as beating the opponent, wanting to impress an audience, or obtaining a big professional contract—are what one is concerned about, then competition is likely to become a distraction, rather than an incentive to focus consciousness on what is happening.*

What a great view of the power of the *other*—*competing*, seeking together to reach the goal. We need the others not to beat them or to prove that we're good to ourselves or someone else, but simply to fuel us for the intrinsic value competition has for our highest purposes. It is seeking your real, authentic, and intrinsic best *in the context of others*. Be it a coach or the swimmer in the next lane, that relational push is required to get Michael Phelps to get to the next level. The other is key to getting better.

So where are we? Well, we have seen in the last chapter that we need the other to stretch us and keep us on track with the small steps, the getting-better steps, in any process of mastery or learning. We've seen that those steps must be internalized and become part of us. Now, since we ended the last chapter with a question, "How do you stay on this well-balanced (Corner Four) diet for the rest of your life?" let's look at the answer now.

STRUCTURE

If you went to college or graduate school, you might have been taken aback the first time you saw a course option for independent study. When you asked your advisor what that was all about, you were told that you could get credit for studying something on your own and having your work overseen by a professor. You would work with him or her to get the topic, direction, objectives, milestones, and requirements, and then you would do it on your own.

"Really?" you asked. "No classes? No course syllabus? No tests?"

"That's right. You're all on your own. By now, you're able to schedule yourself and make sure you're getting it all done. It gives you the freedom to learn what you want to learn, more in your own way."

What a deal, you thought. *I'm in! Sleep in if I want, and still get the credit. Why isn't all of school this way?*

Well, there is a good answer to that. If all of your school had been like that, you wouldn't be able to read or do a lot of other things. You wouldn't have had the advantage of the structure given to you for the first dozen or so years, along with most of your college courses, which built the ability to do it on your own. In other words, independent study is possible only when you've developed the capacity for self-learning, which was internalized from the structure that was given you in all of those other grades and classes. External structure forms us, is internalized, and then becomes internal structure *if* combined with relationship and internalizing experiences. That distinguishes it from simple incarceration. Jail is structure too, but it doesn't build much if it isn't combined with the processes we have talked about throughout this book. It is just external limits.

Sometimes the word *structure* gets a bad rap, but the word actually finds its root in the Latin *struere*, "to build." It is defined by Webster's as "the action of building," or "something arranged in a definite pattern of organization." As a verb, the word means "to construct or arrange according to a plan; give a pattern or organization to."

Wow. Isn't that what we're talking about here—both the what and the how? Improving performance is exactly that. Whether you want to swim faster or become a better leader, you will have to build abilities by arranging them in a definite pattern of organization. And remember Siegel's research here: The mind, formed in relationships, is an organizing, regulating piece of equipment. An internal structure that came from the external structure that relationships provided.

And to structure (build) a mind or other performance capacities, you need a plan. Learning doesn't occur willy-nilly; it has to be

structured well with a solid foundation. When you remodel a building, you put up scaffolding until the new framing and walls are
strong enough to support the roof. When you bake a cake, you pour
the batter in a cake pan to give it form. Whatever you are building,
you have to add an external support to help set the internal structure. Just as an infant gradually forms the internal structures for
self-soothing, so does the cake finally stand firm once it's risen and
molded to the shape of the pan through a series of internal chemical reactions. Getting better occurs through a process of shaping and
forming from the outside, until that ability exists independently of
the source of the structure. Then you can remove the scaffolding. Or
the cake pan, or even the classroom and assignments.

Thus, whenever you embark on the goal of surpassing limits,
you need to consider several factors:

1. What is the ability we are trying to form?

2. What are the ingredients we'll need?

3. What process will we use to form the new structure?

If we're trying to improve the relational skills of a CEO—for
example, the ability to listen, to communicate clearly, or to direct
others—I will work with the client to identify what kinds of information are being communicated in what kinds of relationships,
and what kinds of experiences will impart the desired qualities.
These are the components of the process that we need to structure.
Then there has to be a plan for getting the goal accomplished. We
have to think about how long it will take, how to measure progress,
and how many encounters are required to hit important milestones
along the path.

From research and experience, we know that it takes multiple encounters, a careful sequencing of interactions, delivered at the right moments and in the right amount, for the internalization process to take hold. Michael Phelps didn't become a gold medalist by working with his coach a few times a year, nor will you surpass your limits if you don't commit to making your Corner Four relationships an investment of both time and resources. And the right dosage is important as well, meaning not too little or too much at a time. Phelps didn't swim just one lap, nor five thousand each day. There was a right amount to build the skill.

In my work with clients, I like to use a term I call the growth-structure quotient. It's a synonym for the right dosage, which is the number that's not working plus one. For instance, if I have decided to meet with my writing mentor every two weeks but I'm not getting my homework done right, I add another meeting or interaction to the formula. Instead of meeting every two weeks, now we'll meet every week. If that still doesn't work, then we need to meet even more frequently. It needs to be often enough to help positive patterns form but not so often that the walls of the new internal structure don't have enough time to solidify. I have to have some time to work on it in between.

I have a friend who had been a horrible alcoholic, losing three businesses and a few marriages. By the time I met him, he had been sober for twenty years. He had played an important role in starting recovery movements in many communities. After hearing the legend of his drinking days, I asked him one day, "So, how did you get sober?"

"Oh, it wasn't hard," he said. "I went to three AA meetings a day."

"A *day?*" I asked.

"Yep. My goal was to make it from the end of the morning meeting to the noon meeting without stopping by a liquor store. Then to make it to the evening meeting after that. I did that for quite a while. Then I got stronger, and I went to one a day for a while. Now, twenty years later, I go to a couple a week."

That's exactly what we're talking about. He added the external structure, in the dosage that he needed, and it was internalized over time. If he hadn't been able to make it to noon, he'd have found an extra meeting at ten. The quotient of "what wasn't working plus one."

How much does one need? When I work with CEOs and executives, it varies, but there is one rule I hardly ever violate: there must be some sort of structure. That doesn't mean that it can't change, or isn't variable, but if we don't plan regular meetings, there's usually a problem. Without them, so-called urgent interruptions are all too easy to yield to. If there's unconscious resistance to the work or the challenging moments it might bring, it's far too easy to postpone meetings. The time together must be used for quality work, not just for going through the motions and checking things off a list. I'm talking about the quality of the time as well, not just the number of hours reserved.

I've seen how important this commitment to a schedule can be in my own life. I attended a parent-toddler preschool with each of my daughters. It met from nine to eleven every Wednesday morning. I was excited. What could be better than guaranteed time with them each week: just my daughter and I and the other parent-toddler pairs, mostly moms. I called it my mommies group.

The first week was so cool: a half hour of free play, followed by a half hour on the playground, followed by a half hour in a circle singing toddler songs all together, and then a half hour with the kids eating snacks and the moms and me discussing parenting issues. How do you get them to stay in bed through the night? Potty training. Discipline. Screen usage. How to fire the nanny. (That was a really traumatic situation. The mother decided to get her husband to do the firing, but then he chickened out and actually hired someone else to do it. Amazing.) Anyway, I was all in, set for the year.

The next week, I was at my office, ready to leave to pick up Olivia, when the phone rang. It was a business deal that I was working on, a bit of an urgent situation. I was watching the clock, and then I thought to myself, *This is too important. Livi will never know. She won't even miss it. I'll just take care of this deal this one time, and then we'll be back on next week.* So I took care of my business and didn't worry about it.

The next week, at about eight thirty, another situation came up. I took the phone call and could immediately tell that, again, this was important and would require a lot of my time to sort out. I defaulted to the rationale I'd used the week before. We'll just go next week. But then it hit me like a *hammer.* There would *always* be something important that would come up at the last minute. I realized I had to protect this time with Olivia to build the relationship that I wanted to have with her.

I realized I had to tell the person that I wouldn't be able to continue the call at the moment and that we would have to figure it out later. To be honest, thirteen years later, I can't even remember how the situation turned out (probably just fine), but I do know this:

I treasure incredible memories of going to that class together—as well as with Lucy, her sister, a year and a half later. That shared experience built a foundation between us that I will always cherish.

I learned that structure allows us to invest in the things that are important to us but don't exist inside of us yet. There are plenty of other existing tasks, challenges, and crises that threaten to derail us, but for the things we want to build—for those getting-better goals we want to achieve—we have to create a space and a routine for bringing them into existence. That means replacing old patterns and habits with new ones. Structure helps us do that. I had internalized a pattern of working, doing projects, taking meetings, and doing the work that I needed to do. I did *not* have an internal pattern of taking time out for a daughter back in those early days as a parent. It had to be built from the outside and then internalized. That's what our weekly time together helped structure. Every Wednesday, nine to eleven, period.

If you're trying to grow something new in your head, in a business, or in a relationship, existing patterns in your internal wiring will continue to dominate until there are new ones. And external structure to build them in time and space and defined activities is the only thing that'll give you new ones.

In this instance, the dosage was right for both of us. We did enough other activities together in the in-between times to build on that structured class. With that frequency, the experience was able to grow. Expectations began to be set. We knew how to do it, and the bonding deepened each week. Consistency was critical.

If your Corner Four experiences and activities are well structured, they will build new wiring patterns and capacities in you that you would never have been able to construct on your own. So look at whatever you are trying to build at this moment with your various stakeholders, including yourself. What is the right dosage? What is the right amount of time? How frequently? What has to take place in each dose? As you apply the structure quotient, you will know when something isn't working or not taking hold by adding "one more" until it works. Then you will have found the right dosage. If it doesn't, then you have the wrong medicine (activities), and you'll know at that point. Until you give it its proper due, there's no way to know if it will work or not. But remember, while it is a matter of quantity of time, it's not *only* a matter of time. It's a matter of doing the right activities in the time allotted. That's where the quality in quality of time really comes in. Throw the right information, the right kind of relationship, and the right experience into each dose in a structured pattern, with enough dosage. If you do that, the results might amaze you.

CHAPTER ELEVEN

THE BERMUDA TRIANGLE OF RELATIONSHIPS

Like any other dynamic system, Corner Four relationships need to be nurtured and protected. Just as your body has two systems that keep it healthy—one focused on bringing in and processing nutrients, the other on defending you from infection and toxins—so do strong and resilient Corner Four connections. So far I've discussed the components of a well-balanced Corner Four "diet." In this chapter, I want to bring your attention to some of the bacteria, viruses, and antigens, so to speak, that could put the health of your relationships at risk. You and your Corner Four partners must be able to repel enemy agents by developing an immunity to them, but first you have to be able to name them and surround them with force. Let's look at one of the most pernicious of these "diseases" that can afflict a Corner Four relationship: triangulation.

THE DEADLY TRIAD

I was fascinated by the Bermuda Triangle as a kid. According to the legend, planes and ships were apt to disappear there. Corner Four relationships risk similar outcomes when communication goes into its own dark triangle. I'm talking about a situation in which A should be talking to B but is talking to C *about* B instead. Obviously it will be impossible for A to work out his issues with B if he's not even speaking to her, but that's just the beginning of the problem with this indirect (aka passive-aggressive) style of *non*communication, which I like to call triangulation. The destructiveness of this kind of entanglement is far more troubling. Here's why.

Triangulation sets up something called the victim-persecutor-rescuer (VPR) triad, which I'm calling the Bermuda Triangle of relationships. It works like this. I'm A, you're B, and someone else is C. Let's say I'm bugged with you or disagree with you or don't like the way you recently confronted me. I feel like the victim of something you did to me, and that makes you the persecutor. Therefore, instead of talking directly to you about what's bothering me, I take my hurt feelings to a sympathetic third person, who becomes my "rescuer." I gripe about you, how mean, wrong, abusive, or attacking you were to do what you did or say what you said. I'm not talking to the rescuer for legitimate feedback about our conflict and for help resolving it. That would be a good motivation, but instead, I'm talking to the rescuer just to get validation that I'm right and you're wrong. I want C's support for my side of the argument. It makes me feel better, bleeds off the pain, and helps me avoid talking directly to you.

Talking to a trusted other can often be helpful, but in the VPR scenario, I'm not looking for truth or growth in my conversation with the third party, C. I'm instead looking for that person to rescue me from this mean person (you) and your mean comments, or at least validate *my* view *over* yours. I am looking to feel good. I'm looking for the third party to agree with me, to complain about you, and to reassure me that my feelings are valid. I want C to listen to me as I say, "Can you believe he treated me that way? What right does he have to tell me that, judge me like that?" I want C to agree with me in my hurt and join my anger about what B (you) did. I'm getting that person to be on my side against you. I'm looking for validation, not resolution or growth. I want my rescuer to say, "Wow! You're right! What a jerk he (you) was!"

Have you ever seen this happen in a leadership team? Say there's a meeting, topics are discussed, perspectives are shared, and feedback is given. It sounds as though everyone's on board, right? Then the meeting adjourns, and what do you know? A couple of people gather in the hallway for what is commonly referred to as "the meeting after the meeting." There they are willing to say all sorts of things they wouldn't say to someone directly in the meeting. They have no problem talking trash and looking for another person to side with them when everyone else is out of earshot. They say everything there in the hallway but are never willing to bring their issues back to the room and share them with everyone else—and certainly not with the person they view as responsible for the problem in the first place. Instead, they say to someone else, "Can you believe he really believes that?"

This is not the spirit or the method by which Corner Four relationships will grow. Nor is it the type of communication strategy that someone who wants to overcome current limits should employ.

If I'm mad at you or hurt by you or disagree with you, I (and you) really need me to talk directly to you to resolve it. That's the only way we're going to get to some resolution of the matter. In the absence of that kind of give-and-take, bad feelings fester and spread infection—poisoning not just this one relationship but the mood and positive connections for everyone else involved.

The reason is that triangulation has also now created division between B and C, *who haven't even had a conflict*! Person C now has a one-sided perspective about what happened. Who knows what Person B actually did! C got only one side, which painted B as entirely in the wrong. A's complaints might even be valid, but C can't know without hearing the other side.

Maybe B actually was wrong or hurtful, but because A didn't talk to him, he may not even know why or how he's upset A, so there's no chance that he can address that hurt or change his behavior. Moreover, because A skipped the direct process, he now feels absolutely zero inclination or motivation to look at *his* part in the conflict or to ask how he might also be wrong or maybe could do better. C has "rescued" him from having to consider that possibility by endorsing A's version of what happened and making him feel better. A is totally innocent, according to the rescuer, and therefore A has no impetus to look inward. Even more fixed in his position than before, A's exchange with C also makes him feel morally superior to B.

See what I mean? This is *so* destructive. *Divisiveness is one of the most destructive forces in teams, companies, families, marriages, friendships, and any other relational systems.* It not only prevents resolution, growth, and forward movement, but it also makes problems worse by pitting one person against another and creating further splits throughout the team, family, or organization.

This is how boards, teams, companies, couples, circles of friends, extended families, and other relational systems get sideways with each other and often split or divide forever. The victim and the rescuer, feeling morally superior, decide to leave to form another company, church, or organization. The spouse who feels victimized in the marriage finds an agreeable rescuing ear at the office, gym, or bar. Suddenly he or she feels listened to and understood, validated by this new person, and that just causes even more conflict and division. It happens all the time.

The twist is that often the relationship between the victim and the new rescuer later goes bad as well, as soon as one of *them* feels victimized by the other and finds still *another* rescuer. They have a pattern. Because neither one of them has developed any conflict-resolution skills, they jump from relationship to relationship, job to job, business partner to business partner, church to church, community to community, and so on. With one simple pattern, triangulation, they have managed to keep issues from getting resolved, turn people against each other, prevent individual growth and change, divide organizations, and then infect other situations with that same pattern. Like any cancer, unchecked, it spreads and destroys more and more cells. Persons who use rescuers for validation seldom look at themselves and change. As a result, they repeat the same pattern over and over, destroying relationships, teams, and organizations.

As a person of faith, I'm often reminded of a certain stern passage in the New Testament (Titus 3:10–11). For a long time, I didn't understand what it really meant. On the face of it, it sounds so harsh. It is speaking to the church community and says this: "If people are causing divisions among you, give a first and second warning. After that, have nothing more to do with them. For people like that have turned away from the truth, and their own sins condemn them."

Seems pretty extreme, right? That's what I thought until I became a leadership consultant and spent a few decades working with teams and organizations. I learned something: *divisive people cause more harm than whatever the good things they bring are worth.* If they are truly dividers, they *must* go away. Not because the problem couldn't be fixed—pretty much anything can be worked through if people are willing to do the work, to look hard at themselves and their part in the problem. The real issue is that people who habitually do this are *not* willing to look at themselves and try to resolve things. Instead, they prefer to get people to side with them and agree with them rather than create unity and resolution. I cannot count the number of ugly, dysfunctional situations that I have been called into that finally resolved after the boss asked the divisive troublemaker to leave. People who had formerly been against each other actually found that they liked each other. I've seen one turn to the other and ask, "Wait, why did I hate you? You're a pretty good guy!" I can tell them why: *the divisive person was creating problems and stirring up strife.*

One of the best organizational cultures I know is one that I've had the privilege to do many events with: Ramsey Solutions, Dave Ramsey's company. You might know them through *The Dave Ramsey Show,* the third-largest talk-radio show in North America. There are many reasons for the success and thriving culture that Dave and his team have built, but one of them takes the triangulation issue head-on. The company has a "no-gossip rule." If someone is gossiping about someone instead of talking to that person directly to work it out, the gossiper is given a warning and is then fired if the warning is disregarded. This is a very straightforward, clear, and effective principle. And the cool thing is that this is a culture of healthy debate, high feedback, and quality relationships. Having that rule has made it more than OK for people to speak their minds; it's a necessity if they want to keep their jobs. Who wouldn't want to be part of that kind of Corner Four culture?

THE SOLUTION

The solution for triangulation is to not let it happen anymore, but that takes more than just telling people to stop it. Germs are always in the air; there will always be times when we find ourselves talking to C about B, even if we mean no harm. There are always discussions occurring about someone when they are not in the room. They are often necessary, but some can turn infectious, and that's when we need the immune system to kick in. To stop infection, there are a few important steps.

First, name the problem. Start by talking about the disease of triangulation with the people that it might be affecting. Sometimes people's intent isn't nefarious, but they've found in previous relationships that talking to someone directly hasn't worked. Now they fear it for some reason. Sometimes A and C *will* talk to each other about B, because where they have come from, speaking directly could have been dangerous.

So tell them you've noticed that sometimes there's a meeting after the meeting. At times that can be OK, if it's to do something that is constructive. It can even be constructive to talk with C about B if you're doing so out of a good motive, such as to clarify your thoughts or get advice about how to approach B. Sometimes C can help you gain insight or soothe your hurt so that you can deal with it better. That's not gossip, nor is it divisive *if it's done in the spirit of trying to heal or find resolution*. It all depends on the motive and the effect. If the conversation is in the service of making things better, that is often good.

The problem is that often these sidebar conversations are done not to work it out, but to *avoid* talking to the person directly. You find enough comfort in the sidebar that you no longer feel the need to do anything about it, even when you should. This keeps the person you have the real conflict with from hearing what they need to hear. Or it keeps the rest of the team or family from resolving the issue or turns C against B and clouds the chances of moving forward. So make sure that everyone involved knows why the practice truly is an infection that must be eliminated.

Second, establish a rule or a covenant with each other to help eliminate triangulation from your relationships. Don't do it yourself, and don't participate when someone else offers you the part of the rescuer. Get everyone's agreement to not talk to others about anyone if you wouldn't say or haven't said the same things to that person directly. If you do have an issue with someone, tell him or her directly. Agree that you won't listen to someone gripe about another person either, unless there is some way you can help or encourage them to go to that person directly.

Third, here's where the rubber really meets the road. *You and all the other people in your relationship should agree that, if someone does begin to gossip to you about someone else, you will decline to join in.* Promise instead to ask A, "Have you talked to B about this?" If so, ask what happened, and if you continue to listen, help A work through the issue and form a plan to resolve it. Do not listen and enable someone to just unload on you and get sympathy. Use the conversation to move the issue forward in a good way. Tell A, "I don't feel comfortable talking about B when he's not here. I don't like saying things about someone that I wouldn't say to his face." (As long as it is safe!)

I also like to suggest this sometimes: "Why don't we both go talk to him about it together? I'll offer to help you two think this through. I think that would get us closer to a solution than just talking about it behind his back." I like team members to promise to include everyone. Often all it takes is a sentence. "Let's make sure we bring this point up with the *whole* team" or "Let's make sure everyone's in the room."

When talking directly is problematic or even dangerous or destructive, get clarity on what someone is supposed to do. Go to HR? To a supervisor? To the CEO? I love the example Jim Blanchard set at Synovus by telling all employees to come see him if they have a problem with a boss and can't resolve it.

In issues that are truly one-on-one, always try a direct communication first, A with B, if at all possible. Don't go to C for no good reason. If you can't get resolution, turn to a trusted C to help you instead of a divisive C. I know someone who used to quote Alice Roosevelt Longworth: "If you can't say something good about someone, sit right here by me." She meant it as a joke, but some people are actually like that. They love to be the divisive C; they love gossip.

Fourth, be a good receiver of feedback. If you model the kind of behavior that shows you're open to feedback and willing to listen to other points of view, you may be able to prevent triangulation from starting in the first place. Many times triangulation issues wouldn't exist if person B were easy to talk to. If B is easy to give feedback to, welcomes differing opinions, and isn't defensive, inclined to blame, or otherwise unreceptive to feedback, then A is going to have a much easier time being direct. While we need to be good givers of direct feedback and conversation, we need also to be good receivers as well. I like for team members to help each other understand how they want to be given feedback and to learn how to receive it graciously. Although we mentioned how Ken Blanchard says, "Feedback is the breakfast of champions," we still need to have an appetite for it and receive it well. If people know they can talk to us directly, they'll have less need to go talk to someone else *about* us.

Fifth, build skills—in yourself and in your team. Many times we're asking people to do something they've never been taught to do. They might not have the listening skills, confrontation and conflict skills, negotiation skills, or conversation skills that are needed to have the direct encounters that we're asking them to have. Part of leadership or any Corner Four relationship is helping others grow and get to where they need to be. Remember our discussion earlier on being a stretching agent for each other? Stretch; equip yourself and others with the skills needed to be someone who can have direct conversations about problems. Go take a class yourself.

If you feel you're caught up in a triangle, ask yourself which role you're playing. If you're the offended one talking to a rescuer, stop and say, "You know, thanks for listening, but I really should go talk to B directly. "If you're C, the rescuer, tell A to go talk directly to B, the persecutor, or ask if you can meet both to help them solve the problem. If you're B, the one being talked about, go to A, the gossip, and say, "I heard you have some disagreement with me. How can I help?"

Finally, be wise. Talking about others is not a bad thing. People need to, and love to, talk about each other. "How's your sister doing? What's happening with your team?" Others are frequently the topic of our conversations, and even on the job we must talk about one another and the work we're doing with them, as well as the issues we're having with them. That's normal and good. But, you'll know when it is not divisive. As Supreme Court Justice Potter Stewart once famously wrote in bypassing the vague definition of illegal pornography, "I know it when I see it." The same is true of triangulation. You know it when a conversation is destructive and divisive. You know when a sidebar compartmentalizes a group and keeps issues from being resolved. Don't let it happen. As a leader, remember that you're a steward of your culture.

So let's talk to each other directly. To do that, we need another element in Corner Four relationships: trust. Let's look at what is required for trust to grow.

CHAPTER TWELVE

TRUST

We've examined what it takes to become a high performer. First of all, we've established that, whether we acknowledge it or not, other people have power in one's life that greatly influences one's performance. Second, that power can be positive or negative in its influence. Third, we can't get to the next level without opening ourselves up to the positive power that others bring. We must be an "open system." Fourth, in order to open up and receive, we must be vulnerable and willing to go into a place of need. Fifth, there are certain components that Corner Four relationships provide—fuel, self-control, responsibility and ownership, a realistic positivity about failure, stretches and pushes, steps, structure, and process.

Still, not all high performers are alike. When I work with them, I apply a variety of different tools and methods, depending upon the need. Sometimes a leader needs individual coaching or a sounding board to help think through a challenge. Other times, a team needs to focus on some particular area of growth or development or they need to come together to end some pattern of dysfunction. Although I develop programs, models, and templates, I have never been one of those to act as if one size fits all. I would rather get to know people and then design a plan suited to their particular needs. This approach comes from a deep conviction stated well by the writer of Proverbs 18:13—"Whoever answers before listening is both foolish and shameful."

Now indulge me while I contradict myself. While I do not believe that one size fits all, there are a handful of universal concepts and principles that apply to *every single individual or group performance challenge.* **Trust** is one of those concepts, especially when it comes to tapping into the power of the other. To make an investment in anyone, trust is paramount.

It's hard to argue with the notion that trust is important. Nevertheless, it's not always clear when it's present, what actually builds it, and what it takes to keep it. While I find that everyone values trust, and everyone can feel when it's not there, many times we're not so clear on what it's made of. We don't know how to get to trust. To do so requires that we know what the ingredients are that build trust. So let's take a deeper look into the *anatomy* of trust.

Trust can be defined as a confident expectation. In the same way that we invest in the stock market when we feel confident that we'll see a positive return, so it goes with trust in relationships. We invest ourselves, our time, our energy, our resources, our talents, and so forth when we're confident that doing so will lead to good outcomes. Trust fuels investment—of money, time, energy, and self.

Whom should you trust? In research and experience, I have come to believe that there are five crucial ingredients to look for when you're ready to make such investments.

1. Understanding

2. Intent or Motive

3. Ability

4. Character

5. Track Record

UNDERSTANDING

We trust people who we know understand us, our context, our situation, our needs, what makes it work for us, and what makes it break down. When they truly understand, listen, and care, we are more than willing to open ourselves to them. The highest-performing teams share a deep understanding of each individual's needs as well as a shared understanding of what the group is dealing with and *what it needs from each member to succeed*. Similarly, the highest-performing companies are those whose customers feel that the company really understands their needs and meets them. The best salespeople listen and try to truly understand the customer's context. When the customer feels that "he gets me," he's open to receive and invest.

On the other hand, if people feel we don't get them, their entire system begins to close down, and investment is not forthcoming. I love to study interactions with customer-service people and their customers in those moments when it really matters, like what happens between airline personnel and passengers who are frustrated that something has gone wrong with their trip, or difficult moments in stores, hotels, or hospitals. When you look for this dynamic, you can easily see the difference a positive and understanding connection makes.

The other day, I went to a restaurant in an airport and sat at the counter for about fifteen minutes waiting for service. I tried to catch the attention of one of the servers but never could. Finally I looked at my watch and realized that I wasn't going to have enough time to get my food and still make my flight, so I got up to leave. At that point, the person working behind the counter asked me if everything was good, and I said, "Actually, no. I've been waiting so long for service that now I don't have enough time."

Immediately, he said, "Well, you should have come up and found one of us. You shouldn't have just waited. We would have gotten you something if you had come up and told us."

"OK, thanks," I said. I didn't say, "Oh . . . you're right. I write books on taking responsibility and being proactive, and there's no doubt about it. This is my fault. Thanks for telling me. I should have come and gotten you. I shouldn't have been working on my computer and let the time get away. Thank you for the life lesson. I'll always remember it: I am existentially responsible for my life." But I wanted to.

Of course, he was right. I could have tracked down a server and probably should have, but for whatever reason, I didn't, and I didn't get service, no matter whose fault it was. Even though I was somewhat to blame, his response didn't make me trust that the next time I went there I would be treated well.

This exchange is, unfortunately, all too typical. The person tries to devalue what the customer is saying and then scolds the customer for doing something wrong or not knowing better. So much for that.

I wanted to say some other not-so-nice things, but I kept walking. Just at that moment, another server noticed me leaving, and when she asked how everything was, I told her the same thing. She said, "Oh no! That's so frustrating. I'm sorry that happened. We are kind of swamped and overwhelmed right now, and that is a bummer. Sorry we missed you."

All of a sudden, my mood shifted. Someone had understood. That's pretty much all I needed. This was the kind of person I'd be willing to trust—and the kind of customer-service experience that would make me willing to give this place another try . . . as long as the first guy was not there.

I get why it's so hard for us to operate this way. Too often we're overly concerned with ourselves, too much so to *take a moment* to really understand what's going on with someone else, and make sure they know that we understand. I often say to leaders, "You don't understand your people or your customers when you understand them. You understand them when they *understand* that you understand." That's when you know you have trust.

My work with companies often entails a certain kind of project that I absolutely love. It involves helping a company improve working relations between the home office and some part of the field. Whether branches, retail outlets, franchises, clinics, or distributors, it's a matter of relationships and thus subject to all the dynamics that make relationships good or bad.

There are several reasons I love that kind of work, some of it purely intellectual and professional. It gives me the opportunity to dissect the physics of performance in that kind of structure. And I love to figure out how the relationship is creating or distracting from Corner Four connections and from performance results. As with individual executives, I love to see these groups build unity and surpass their limits. It's a passion for me.

In most relationship issues, there are two sides of the story. And it's fascinating to figure that out, and it's satisfying to see the tangible results—more revenue, more profit, more engagement, better culture and development in people, and so forth. But seeing how the human relationships grow and deepen is even more fulfilling. As I've argued throughout this book, you really can't get the one, sustained high performance, without the other—deep, connected relationships.

When everything goes well with these kinds of projects, the field-office people develop a much higher level of trust in the home office because *they feel better understood*. The fact that the CEO or other high-ranking leader actually listens to them—on "listening tours," for example—starts a chain of events that builds newfound levels of trust. You hear things like, "I trust you because you've shown that you care enough to listen and see what it's truly like for me."

So just listen, listen, listen. It's the right place to start. For instance:

- A spouse finally listens to his mate's pain and complaints and the effects his behavior is having on the relationship. Instead of being defensive, devaluing, or explaining the other person's pain away, he truly gets it.

- Instead of just telling a teenager how he's falling short, parents sit down with their child and listen to him explain what his days are really like, what kinds of challenges he's facing in school and in his social circle, what kinds of joys and frustrations are contributing to the situation. They ask questions, and then they listen, rather than immediately lecturing and making demands.

- An executive team goes around the circle and listens to each member explain the difficulties that one department is causing for the other, usually when they don't even know it, and how the way they work makes it hard for the other group to do what they need to do.

- A leader, instead of just giving direction and orders, takes the time to understand all that's involved in pulling off what she is asking her team to do. She listens as the team recounts the pros and cons of different approaches and demonstrates that she recognizes the risks and the demands her goals will require to be met.

- Company reps sit down with customers and other stakeholders to hear their stories about using the service or the product. But more than that, they learn about their lives in general, what's important to them, where their struggles are, and what they value most.

These are all examples of putting your trust where your mouth is, so to speak. In fact, you could even get elected president of the United States just by doing a little more listening. Remember the

1992 election when Bill Clinton went around the country just listening? He had one line: "I feel your pain." Politics aside, it worked. Voters felt that he understood their lives and their values. He connected with them. The contrast was stark when the sitting president George H. W. Bush was asked by a voter how much a gallon of milk cost and he didn't know. Even though he may have very well been just as caring and compassionate as Bill Clinton, that incident made people feel that he was too disconnected from them, that he didn't understand what life was like for regular citizens. The voters felt that Clinton understood them better, just from listening and empathizing. That impression never really went away.

This is often the case. *Good, caring people can be perceived wrongly by others simply because a connection has not been made.* As a leader, a spouse, a colleague, and a parent, take time to ask yourself: Have I shown the people I want to have a Corner Four relationship with that I truly am listening, that I understand them? And, before you invest your trust in someone else, ask yourself if you feel that they are listening and truly understand where you're coming from. I will rarely invest in or with someone who can't listen.

INTENT AND MOTIVE

Whenever we meet someone—especially a stranger but also a friend, a boss we see every day, or even a family member—we unconsciously scan the face, read the body language, and assess the tone of voice to determine whether the person is with us or against us. It's just what humans do. Remember that fight-or-flight instinct? Trust is the salve that calms that itch. If we think someone is in our corner, we assume that what they say and what they do will be said and done to help us.

When we find people who seem to truly understand us, next we need to know their *motives*. What's driving them in this relationship? Are they in it only for themselves and their interests, or do they care about ours as well? We trust people when we know that their motives are good, that they want good things for us, even if at times it might cost them. Good relationships are built on this bedrock of trust: I know that you want the best for me, so I trust you.

We tend to think in terms of people's motives being either good or bad—either for us or against us—but a lot of times, people are just neutral toward us. Basically they are just innocently looking out for themselves. There's nothing wrong with that per se, but when we're looking to invest ourselves in a relationship, *neutrality is never enough*. We need the people we trust to be more than neutral. We need for them to be our allies, champions, and helpers! Corner Four demands more than neutrality or simple fairness: it demands that we treat each other *better* than neutrally. It means that we are treating each other in a way that shows we are for each other's good.

Following the Golden Rule, we need to treat others as we want to be treated. It is easy to treat people well when they're treating us well or performing well, but that's just neutral and fair. Mafiosi do that. We need the people we trust to be on our team and helping us even when we fail them, make a mistake, or drop the ball. Fairness says they could hurt us back, an eye for an eye, but a Corner Four person would ask, "What's going on? How can I help?" In

Corner Four, we give back better than we might be getting on any particular day, even when there's nothing in it for us. We are still for their best.

When we feel that certain people want the best for us, we invest in them. We trust them. If you sense that a certain doctor cares about your health more than your bill, you invest in that doctor's guidance. I recently did a consult with a health-care company that had a practice of calling customers who hadn't been in for their regular checkup—because their mission was to keep people healthy. But, I also have had experience with health-care systems that call patients to remind them of appointments just to drive revenues. I can literally feel the difference in motive. I much prefer the first—and, by the way, that company's profits were very, very good. People trusted it with their health for a long time because they felt it cared.

I recently led a retreat for an executive team in a technology company. I asked each person to provide a rating on how much they felt that the rest of the team was for them, for their department, for their interests. There were seven members, and all of them gave the team either a 4 or a 5 (on a scale of 1 to 5)—except for one person. He gave the team a 1. Ouch. That's a big problem. One of their most significant members had lost trust. He felt that everyone else was completely uninterested in helping him succeed. If we hadn't discovered that, his discontent would have gotten worse. They *had* to fix that in order to move forward.

Is your company for you? If you're a leader, do your people know that you're for them? Your kids? Spouse? I presume that you are, but if you want trust to flourish, you have to make sure that they know it as well.

ABILITY

It's easy to get caught up in the good feelings that trust engenders, but trust without commensurate levels of ability isn't enough either.

Someone may have remarkable compassion and empathy for you, and pure motives, but you can trust only if that person has the *ability* to do what you need done. A friend can comfort you and fluff your pillows when you've broken your leg, but you wouldn't ask a friend without medical training to surgically repair the break. You'd want an orthopedic surgeon.

It shouldn't be taken as a put-down to question another person's ability. It's *not* personal. In fact, it's a sign of strength when a team has enough trust that members can ask each other whether they have all the capabilities it will take to launch a new product or set out on a new strategic path. I am heartened when I work with a team or an individual leader with the kind of relationships that make it possible for these conversations to occur. They can honestly question one another's abilities to make sure they're capable before they launch something. Perhaps you say to the marketing department, "I'm not feeling secure that you guys have the capacity to launch this new campaign with all of the other things you have going on. Help me get there." That's real Corner Four communicating, not an insult.

After all, the point is to actually deliver on what we set out to do for someone, right? Why wouldn't you want to have the best chance of succeeding—whether you're talking about your business, your marriage, or your role as a parent? If you have embraced that growth mind-set, it's only natural to ask each other whether you have absolutely everything it takes to proceed—and to trust that your Corner Four relationship partners will expect that kind of candor as well.

All too often, when people start a new business or a mission-driven nonprofit, they tend to put people on their board whom they know and like. There's nothing wrong with that, so long as they also have the needed skills. So, ask not just how good people are, but also if they can do what you need them to do in this relationship.

Ability is key to trust. We want to know our pilots have flown before. We want to know our surgeons have cut before, and the patient woke up. We want to know the fund manager can make a return on assets. Otherwise we're not trusting at all; we're gambling. Trust, as noted earlier, is a "confident expectation" that someone can deliver. Ability drives that expectation and confidence in it.

CHARACTER

I am amazed by how easy it is for people to overlook the importance of character—and to not really grasp its full meaning. The dictionary even does a more thorough job of defining the word than we do in evaluating people. Merriam-Webster.com defines it this way: "the way someone thinks, feels and behaves: someone's personality."

Too often we think of character strictly in moral terms: Is this person honest and ethical? But character is much more than whether or not someone is going to lie, cheat, or steal. Those are merely "permission to play" character traits. Anyone who's dishonest or tries to cheat you or steal shouldn't even be under consideration for your trust. Run away, and keep your hands on your wallet and your heart. That's elementary.

I'm talking about other character traits beyond honesty and ethics: Optimist or pessimist? Proactive or passive? Does she persevere and solve problems when things get difficult? Is he too soft for what you need? Too hard? Too rigid? Too impulsive? Too paralyzed by fear of failure? Compassionate? Kind? Brittle? Fun? Resilient? Forgiving? We could go on and on.

But consider this. An individual could have everything we have discussed so far about trust. He or she could be understanding, have good motives, have high ability, and still lack an essential character trait that is needed in your context before you can trust. For instance, what if it's someone who needs a lot of validation and positive feedback, and yet you're going to ask him to take over a failing entity and turn it around? There is not going to be a lot of good news for quite a while. If someone thrives only on positive results, he might not have the staying power for a turnaround. He's a good person, but his character (not moral, but how he is put together) isn't a good fit for this particular job.

The higher you go in organizations, the more important questions of character and emotional intelligence become. Research and the daily headlines from the front page of the *Wall Street Journal* bear that out. At a certain level in leadership, everyone is smart, experienced, and highly capable; those traits are no longer the differentiators. Individual character is the big differentiator. It's leaders' emotional, cognitive, and interpersonal skills—not just what they can *do*, but *how* they do it. Character determines whether they inspire others to trust them.

TRACK RECORD

People's minds make maps in order to negotiate the world. Your mind and mine are always constructing schemata—diagrams or maps—so we know what to do next. Just like a real map, these mental maps help us navigate relationships, sort incoming data, make decisions, and prioritize effort. They also show us what we can expect.

The same thing is true as our minds are deciding whether or not we can trust a person. Everyone has a mental map of what one can expect from a person: the last time. "The last time I asked you to show up and deliver what I needed, you did. So I feel comfortable going down that road again."

Unless you didn't. Then the map shows lots of red flags and stop signs as you approach the trust intersection. We often see these warning signs, but just as often we ignore the signals of trouble. We're often told to give people the benefit of the doubt, and that's a noble intention. But when we've been down the road with someone before and know that it was potholed and filled with dead man's curves, then we have only ourselves to blame if we jump back into the car with them. Before you do that again, ask yourself, "What would be *different* about this time? What would have to *change* for me to trust this person this time?" Of course, extenuating circumstances sometimes intervene. Everyone has an off day or experiences a crisis that might limit performance for a time. Stuff happens. Don't jump to conclusions without taking a longer view of a person's track record. Look not just at the most recent time, but at the broad pattern to determine whether you're dealing with a blip in an otherwise excellent record. The "last time" schema is more about the whole record than one anomaly.

Remember, the best predictor of the future is the past, unless there is something new and different in the picture. If the track record has been poor but you're thinking of trusting someone, have a very good reason to take that step. If you're trusting him to be nice to you now, has he gone to a year of anger management classes? If you're trusting him to lead you but his past leadership was poor, has he had some leadership coaching? If you are trusting her to be a confidant and help you through a tough time, how did she respond to you in the past when you confided in her and looked to her for encouragement? What happened the last time you opened up to her about a problem? Did she listen or just get on your case for having a problem in the first place? Or did she ignore it and change the subject, unable to process something more painful? If those were true, what is there that is new or different this time?

So whom should you trust? It depends! Reread the previous pages, and don't be afraid to question your first impulse next time you have to decide where to bank your trust. As they say on Wall Street (at least they should!) and in all securities advertisements, investor beware!

NICE GUYS DON'T FINISH LAST

I had a very interesting conversation recently with a leader who accomplishes a lot and is very driven and effective. I have always been a fan of his work. We were working on a project together, and he made a reference to a particular work habit of his, logging almost every thought he has about his work into a very complicated matrix in a journal, and I asked him about it. Nothing wrong with carrying a little book around and jotting down good ideas when they come. But this was much more; it was obsessive. He said, "I think it's probably part of my anxiety disorder."

I inquired more, and he told me that he had been managing a significant anxiety disorder for some time and had relied on a number of tricks and habits to keep it in check. As I listened, I couldn't help being moved by how much effort it must cost and how distressing it must be for him to manage this condition. I also couldn't help wondering how much better his life and work could be if he didn't have to do all that. The psychologist in me had to speak up.

"So, . . . I'm just curious. You know, what you're experiencing is treatable. Anxiety disorders are pretty fixable. You don't have to suffer with this—really," I said. "Why don't you get some help for this?"

"I would," he said, "but I am afraid to."

"Afraid of what?" I asked.

"Afraid that I wouldn't be as effective," he said. "I've always thought that the anxiety I have about something possibly going wrong or not working is what makes me so good at what I do. I always make sure, and double make sure, everything is covered and nothing can possibly go wrong. I feel like if I weren't anxious, I would miss a lot of things and there wouldn't be the same results."

"Wow!" I said. "I wonder how people without anxiety disorders ever accomplish anything." I was joking—sort of, but not really. But he didn't quite get it.

"I don't know," he said. "I'd fear that I couldn't perform at the same level if I didn't have the anxiety."

Incredible, I thought. Still, I've heard some version of this explanation many times before and in many different kinds of situations. For example, often when I give a talk about how leadership, character, emotional intelligence, and relational issues affect results, I invariably get a question like this: "You are saying that all of this relational ability is important for leadership and getting results, and being successful. But what about someone like Steve Jobs? He was very successful and known to be difficult to work with in some of these ways. How do you explain that? It seems like it's the hard-driving, dominating behavior that gets some people where they are. It's always the jerks that are most successful."

Or consider an e-mail I recently received from a well-known national news commentator who in her reporting continues to run into powerful and successful people who are "not good guys," as she put it. She'd sent me a link to an article concluding that "mean" people and "jerks" tend to be more successful than the "nice guys" in all areas of business, entertainment, and other fields. Her comment about the article was this: "This is depressing. Do you agree with this? I am starting to believe it, based on my experience."

Both of these examples underscore the same false assumption: *the myth that something dysfunctional is contributing to success.* You've heard it too with comments like this: "He's such a jerk, but I guess that's how he got to where he is." Or even: "If I were more of a shrew at work, I probably would be running this company."

Trust me. Neither statement is true. Being a jerk, or a narcissist, or having an anxiety disorder that drives one to double-check everything—these are not the personality traits that make for great success. Remember, there are also an awful lot of unsuccessful jerks, narcissists, screamers, and people with anxiety disorders. And there are a lot of very effective, successful people who have none of those maladies.

The truth is that Steve Jobs was successful because of incredible talent, brains, vision, marketing abilities, design strengths, charm, and initiative. He was assertive, he had amazing reservoirs of creative energy, and he didn't hesitate to push people to their limits and beyond. These are all *positive* attributes that made him successful.

The jerk behavior just got in the way, unless you think getting fired, losing key people and relationships, and creating sometimes toxic environments are the recipe for an iPhone. It was *not* the oppressive, domineering behavior that made it all work. Apple worked *in spite of it* and probably could have been even more outstanding without it. What if he had never gotten fired? What might the company have done if he'd been less difficult?

Mark these words: *Nice guys do not finish last, and jerks do not finish first. Great performers finish first, and if they are great and good people, they do even better.*

As research confirms, the qualities that lead to great performance are only enhanced in great relationships. The opposite is also true: great performance qualities are either limited or reduced by dysfunctional relationships. On page 5 of *Working Together: Why Great Partnerships Succeed* (HarperCollins, 2010), former Disney CEO Michael Eisner reminisced about his longtime business partner:

> *We were headed into the toughest challenge of our professional lives, together. For the next ten years, that journey would be as exciting, enjoyable, rewarding, and triumphant as either of us could have dared to hope. From our first day in the office that fall, my partnership with Frank Wells taught me what it was like to work with somebody who not only protected the organization but protected me, advised me, supported me, and did it all completely selflessly. I'd like to think I did the same for Frank, as well as the company. We grew together, learned together, and discovered together how to turn what was in retrospect a small business into indeed a very big business. We learned that one plus one adds up to a lot more than two. We learned just how rewarding working together can be.*

I love those words: protected, advised, supported, selfless, grew, learn, discover, rewarding. Your life, performance, health, well-being, and pretty much everything you value depends on the power that the other brings to the table. This is serious stuff. It's not for jerks.

Do not fear the health of Corner Four. Being supported, challenged, and grown into your best person by great relationships will not undermine your success, only advance it. Being that kind of growth agent for others will only enhance their lives and yours. In the end, only Corner Four people are left standing. The others will fall, fail, or fade.

It behooves us all to look for and build the kinds of connection that Corner Four people embody, and become that kind of connector ourselves:

- Connection that fuels

- Connection that gives freedom

- Connection that requires responsibility

- Connection that defangs failure and learning

- Connection that challenges and pushes

- Connection that builds structure

- Connection that unites instead of divides

- Connection that is trustworthy

As you go through the routines of your life—meeting with colleagues, catching up with family at holidays, having dinner with friends, or taking walks with your spouse, don't be afraid to check your own internal GPS to see how it's going. Where are you? Are you lonely in Corner One? Are you feeling crappy in Corner Two? Are you experiencing a fleeting thrill in Corner Three? Or are you feeling protected, advised, supported, and rewarded in Corner Four? Which corner are you in? And who is in that corner with you?

The answer to those questions will determine whether or not you get past your current limit, even all the way to your dream. I hope you find Corner Four, live there as much as possible, and out-perform even your wildest dreams.

ACKNOWLEDGMENTS

Sometimes people ask me, "How long does it take you to write a book?" I usually say, "It takes several years to write it . . . and then I have to write it down." The process of this book was more like that than probably any of my previous books. If I were really to acknowledge the people who helped with getting this book done, I would have to list all of the others in my life who have been the kind of positive power that has helped, healed, taught, supported, and saved me for so many years . . . starting very young. So I won't list all of those who participated in the "years to write it" and will thank only a few who were key in the "writing it down" phase of the last year. The "others" (from friends and family to coaches, mentors, teachers, and healers) know who they are . . . and I am very thankful for them.

In the writing process, I have to thank my publisher Hollis Heimbouch who really, really helped me get these constructs finally onto paper. She made a special effort to get me to download what feels like decades of work and then helped me think through how to organize it into what I hope you, the reader, find to be a helpful form. Thanks, Hollis. And thanks to Stephanie at Harper as well, for keeping the ball moving.

Also, thanks to my agents, Jan Miller and Shannon Miser-Marven from Dupree Miller, who helped get the project from an idea through the publishing matrix. I will always feel grateful to be working with the best literary agents in the world. You rock.

And to my immediate team who helped keep all the balls in the air in all of our other work while I was "writing it down." Your work in the last year has been amazing in getting these concepts out there in social media and other platforms to help as many people as possible. Thank you Jennifer, Lexi, Jayson, Gina, and Greg.

And the crew at CTR who tirelessly pour themselves into the lives of others: Maureen, Lisa, Christine, Jodi, and Patti.

Then, always, thanks to my friends and family. You make life what it is for me.

INDEX

ABOUT THE AUTHOR

Dr. Henry Cloud is an acclaimed leadership expert, psychologist, and *New York Times* bestselling author whose books have sold over 10 million copies. In 2014, *Success* magazine named Dr. Cloud one of the top 25 most influential leaders in personal growth and development. He graduated from Southern Methodist University with a BS in psychology and completed his PhD in clinical psychology at Biola University.